DATE DUE

DEC 2			
FEB 7			
FEB 2 8 '90			

LENDING POLICY

IF YOU DAMAGE OR LOSE LIBRARY
MATERIALS, THEN YOU WILL BE
CHARGED FOR REPLACEMENT. FAIL-
URE TO PAY AFFECTS LIBRARY
PRIVILEGES, GRADES, TRANSCRIPTS,
DIPLOMAS, AND REGISTRATION
PRIVILEGES OR ANY COMBINATION
THEREOF.

DEMCO

The Rich and the Poor
in
Supreme Court History
1790 - 1982

by Russell Galloway

Paradigm Press

ISBN 0-937572-01-2

Library of Congress Cataloging in Publication Data

Galloway, Russell.
   The rich and the poor in Supreme Court history, 1790–1982.

   Includes bibliographical references and index.
   1. United States. Supreme Court. 2. Law and politics. 3. Judicial process--United States. 4. Equality before the law--United States. I. Title.
KF8742.G26 1983   347.73'26'09   82-62643
ISBN 0-937572-01-2   347.3073509

Paradigm Press
127 Greenbrae Boardwalk
Greenbrae, California
94904

To my children, Mark, Kit,
Katie, and Ben

ACKNOWLEDGMENTS

Several groups and individuals are entitled to special thanks for aiding in the creation of this book. First, my clients and colleagues at Legal Aid Society of Alameda County, who taught me about the treatment - and often mistreatment - of the poor by the legal system. They provided the original stimulus to undertake a systematic study of the fortunes of the rich and the poor at the bar of the Supreme Court. Second, my students and colleagues at University of Santa Clara School of Law, who provided important feedback that led to major revisions and improvements of earlier drafts. Third, Hal Aigner, of Paradigm Press, who gave both encouragement and many good suggestions that strengthened the final manuscript. Fourth, Margie Marumoto, who contributed cheerful and exceptionally able help in moving the manuscript through the many revisions. Finally, my wife and children, who gave me support and encouragement needed to keep the project moving despite many delays, set-backs, and discouragements. Thanks to all of you.

R.G.

The publisher offers special thanks to Dr. Henry Aigner, Sandy Abbot, Kathy Geiger, Marge Sierra, and Pat Werner for their continued support of Paradigm Press, and to Bill Henkin for suggestions made during the formative stages of this book's development.

H.A.

Contents

Part Four

The Second Conservative Era (1890-1937)

Part Five

The Second Liberal Era (1937-1969)

Part Six

The Third Conservative Era (1969-   )

Preface

The liberal-activist United States Supreme Court that spearheaded many of the egalitarian revolutions in the 1960's is now a rapidly fading memory. With its waning, a distinctive period of liberal jurisprudence has apparently drawn to a close as such formidable and frequently controversial figures as Justices Earl Warren (1953-69),* Hugo Black (1937-71), and William O. Douglas (1939-75) have in their turn retired from the Bench.

Their resignations have opened up the opportunity for a Court of a markedly different character to emerge. In keeping with the contemporary shift toward conservative viewpoints throughout the executive and legislative branches of the federal government, subsequent appointments of new Justices have presented to the nation jurists of a political bent opposite to that embraced by their immediate forebears.

The shift from a liberal to a conservative Supreme Court continues to this day. The 1981 selection of Arizona's Sandra Day O'Connor to fill the seat vacated by the moderate-conservative Potter Stewart (1958-81) was the sixth consecutive appointment by a Republican President and, to all appearances, the sixth consecutive occasion on which an appointee has been more conservative in outlook than the Justice he or she has replaced.

---

* When a Justice is introduced for the first time, his or her tenure on the Court will be indicated in parentheses.

i

In its role as arbiter, the conservative Bench will decide numerous controversies of profound importance to the ongoing struggle for a just society. With their power to establish the procedural rules that control access of the rich and the poor alike to judicial remedies for alleged wrongs, and with their responsibility to interpret federal constitutional and statutory rules regulating economic affairs, the nine Justices sit in a society rife with debate over a variety of economic concerns including public welfare programs, low-cost housing subsidies, labor law, antitrust law, consumer protection, social security, and equal employment opportunity. And as has happened in other times and with other issues, the final word in many of these debates will be delivered in the form of a Supreme Court ruling.

At present, the Bench's overall economic posture favors the rich. Increasingly, the nation faces the prospect of a Supreme Court entirely without a liberal wing. Groups such as the poor, the disadvantaged, and the unorganized, who have previously looked to the Supreme Court as a bastion of hope, may soon confront an assembly of Justices whose life experiences and natural inclinations lead them to respond sympathetically to financially powerful individual and corporate interests. As a result, the legal contest perennially waged between the rich and the poor has now been thrown into stark relief against a conservative judicial background, with the salient details of the drama to be filled in by future decisions.

And this shift toward increased conservatism will likely continue for several more years to come. The Court's two remaining liberals, William J. Brennan (1956-), age 76, and Thurgood Marshall (1967-), age 74, have been plagued by poor health and may have to resign before the end of the Reagan presidency. Moreover, the conservative Reagan well may enjoy the opportunity to select younger jurists to replace as many as three members of the current Court's dominant conservative wing. Warren E. Burger (1969-), the Court's hard-line conservative Chief Justice, and Lewis F. Powell Jr. (1972-), a former corporate lawyer and intellectual leader of the Bench's right wing, have both reached age 75. Harry A. Blackmun (1970-), the most moderate of Richard Nixon's four appointees, is now 74. In short, as all of these Justices may choose to retire in the near future, a Court comprised of six or more Reagan appointees is presently a very real possibility.

The United States Supreme Court, then, has entered into another conservative era, the third in its history. As in the first such era, which was established by the Federalists and lasted from 1790 to 1835, and the second, which was characterized by the ascendancy of laissez faire economic policies and lasted from 1890 to 1937, the Court has come under the dominance of economic conservatives who tend to side with the rich and the powerful in the perennial socio-economic battle between classes over the distribution of wealth.

The transition has been one of enormous potential consequence. Sooner than later, a Reagan Court, as all Supreme Courts must, will exercise its vast powers over matters bearing, to one degree or another, on the single issue that gives the terms "economic conservative" and "economic liberal" their central meaning. That is, a Reagan Court will find itself, as all Supreme Courts do, acting as an arbiter of conflicts between this country's wealthy and its needy.

The material that follows attempts to illuminate the nature of the United States Supreme Court and its historical role in political economics. Over the course of nearly two centuries, a large number of seemingly isolated issues brought to the Court's attention have turned out to be tied to a single theme, namely the competing interests of the wealthy and the needy. Much may be learned about both the Supreme Court and the American system of "justice" through the study of how different Justices have reacted to this enduring contest between the rich and the poor.

Part One

The Court And The Constitution

Chapter One

The Supreme Court's Role
In Economic Controversy

The United States Supreme Court was created in 1789 pursuant to article III, section 1 of the federal Constitution, which provides, "The judicial Power of the United States, shall be vested in one supreme Court, and in such inferior Courts as the Congress may from time to time ordain and establish." Justices are nominated by the President and must be confirmed by the Senate. As further provided in the Constitution, Justices may serve as long as they wish "during good Behavior." Should misbehavior arise within their ranks, Justices may be removed from office only through impeachment proceedings conducted by the United States Senate. The number of Justices serving at any one time may be altered by statute. Over the years, the Court's size has fluctuated from six to ten members before settling in 1877 on the current number of nine.

Since its inception, the Supreme Court has been invested with the authority to affirm or reverse decisions made by lower federal and state courts. For approximately its first 135 years, exercise of this authority was legally mandated over a wide range of cases. But since 1925, the Court has enjoyed nearly complete discretion in selecting the cases it will hear. When evaluating requests for review of lower court actions, the Court is primarily concerned with questions of social or legal importance rather than questions of justice in individual cases.

7

On acceptance of a case for full review, attorneys representing both sides of the issue at bar attempt to persuade the Justices to rule in their favor. In the process, they present to the Court written briefs containing references to appropriate authorities, including relevant constitutional mandates, prior case decisions — i.e, precedent — statutory and administrative directives. In both briefs and subsequent oral arguments, the attorneys formulate an interpretation of the material cited, with each side hoping that the Justices will endorse its viewpoint. Some while later, normally seven months, the Court releases a written response, that is additionally read publicly. The response recounts the majority opinion in the case and is accompanied by any concurring and dissenting opinions.

Given that the Supreme Court is constrained by such legal authority as the Constitution, statutes, and case law, one may wonder how the Justices' treatment of the rich and the poor has been able to vary sufficiently to warrant anything more than cursory attention. The central reality of the situation, however, is that interpretation is an enormously flexible process. The Justices, in fact, possess a great deal of freedom to write their personal preferences on an issue into any opinion. Moreover, they ordinarily enjoy the "sovereign prerogative of choice" and may set precedent aside and create new case law when they wish. Hence, the controlling factor in many cases brought before the Bench is simply the Justices' own perceptions of whatever outcome they consider to be best.

When a vacancy appears on the United States Supreme Court, generally by reason of death or retirement, the attitudes of the President responsible for filling the empty seat become of paramount importance in the selection of the new Justice. It is not surprising, then, that the economic, political, and social philosophies held by a nominee play a major role in the appointment process. Throughout the country's history, Presidents have usually been acutely aware of the Court's great power to interpret the law. As a result, these Chief Executives have sought to appoint jurists whose policy views most closely accord with their own. In most instances, the Senate has approved these appointments quickly and methodically.

With the founding of the Republic, George Washington, for example, initiated the first conservative era of Supreme Court history by selecting conservative Federalists to fill all of the Bench's original six seats. Andrew Jackson later reversed that pattern and initiated the Court's first liberal era, lasting roughly from 1836 to 1890, by appointing Justices who shared the populist sympathies of Jacksonian democracy. In the early 1920's, Warren Harding prolonged the Court's second conservative era, which lasted from 1890 to 1937, by choosing four conservative Justices to fill vacancies on the Bench. Franklin D. Roosevelt, in his turn, brought on the Court's second liberal era, 1937 to 1969, with his appointment of eight fellow New Dealers to the Court. Under Richard Nixon, the third conservative era commenced, an epoch that is likely to continue through the Reagan administration and for many years beyond.

From 1790 to the present, several images regarding the Court's attitudes toward the rich and the poor have emerged. Some commentators say that the Court predominantly serves the corporate rich and typically decides cases in their favor. Others contend that the Court too often champions the poor and strives to protect the little person from exploitation. Still others claim that the Court usually acts neutrally to balance competing interests and to apply justice impartially. All parties agree, however, that the Court's duties include - because government's duties include - the responsibility to serve as a mediator of clashes between citizens of wealth and power and those bereft of such amenities.

From the best evidence of the past, the struggle between the rich and the poor has endured at least since the days during which recorded history began. As the famous American historian George Bancroft put it, "The feud between...the house of Have and the house of Want, is as old as social union, and can never be entirely quieted."[1] In the American 1700's, the rich-poor issue carried over into the formation of the United States in a fashion so pervasive that many theorists consider it the most fundamental of all the Republic's early controversies. Clear recognition of the conflict's primacy in American governmental affairs can easily be traced back to the time of the Constitution's formulation.

---

1. Quoted in Arthur M. Schlesinger, Jr., *The Age of Jackson*, (Boston: Little, Brown & Co., 1945), frontispiece.

A classic articulation of the rich-poor controversy was provided in Number 10 of *The Federalist*. There James Madison, principal author of the Constitution's Bill of Rights, the nation's fourth President, and a founding father, wrote:

> *The most common and durable source of factions has been the various and unequal distribution of property. Those who hold and those who are without property have ever formed distinct interests in society. Those who are creditors, and those who are debtors, fall under a like discrimination.... The regulation of these various and interfering interests forms the principal task of modern legislation, and involves the spirit of party faction in the necessary and ordinary operations of the government.*

Alexander Hamilton, the "prime minister" of the Washington administration and one of Madison's few intellectual equals among the founding fathers, completely agreed with his peer's contention and further asserted that the conflict between the wealthy and the needy should be the basic determinant of the very structure of government. According to Hamilton:

> *All communities divide themselves into the few and the many. The first are the rich and well born, the other the mass of people. The voice of the people has been said to be the voice of God; and however generally this maxim has been quoted and believed, it is not true in fact. The people are turbulent and changing; they seldom judge or determine right. Give therefore to the first class a distinct, permanent share in the government. They will check the unsteadiness of the second....*[2]

America's second President, John Adams, whose understanding of political history and theory matched that of Madison

---

2. Quoted in Charles A. Beard, *An Economic Interpretation of the Constitution of the United States* (New York: The Free Press, 1913), at 199. Hereafter referred to as Beard, *Constitution.*

and Hamilton, developed one of the most complete expositions of the rich-poor issue as it pertained to the nation's formative years.[3] From Adams' viewpoint, politics are founded directly upon economic interests. Society, he contended, is everywhere divided into two classes, a small group of rich persons and a large mass of poor. Further, he held, these classes are engaged in constant struggle, with the rich seeking to augment their possessions at the expense of the poor and with the poor seeking to despoil the rich. The primary function of the government, then, is to mediate this struggle so that relative justice is done to all.

As a background to his commentaries on the Jeffersonian era, historian Charles Beard described Adams' economic and political thought in this way:

> *Adams' system of political science may be summed up in the following manner:*
>
> *1. Society is divided into contending classes, of which the most important and striking are the gentlemen and the common people, or to speak in economic terms, the rich and the poor.*
>
> *2. The passion for the acquisition of property or the augmentation of already acquired property is so great as to over-ride considerations arising out of religious or moral sentiments.*
>
> *3. Inevitably the rich will labor to increase their riches at the expense of the poor, and if unchecked, will probably on account of superior ingenuity and wisdom, absorb nearly all of the wealth of the country.*
>
> *4. Out of the contest for economic goods arise great political contests in society, particularly between the rich and the poor....*
>
> *8. Therefore, the constitution must embody in it a representation of the rich and poor as distinct orders;*

---

3. John Adams, *A Defense of the Constitution of Government of the United States of America against the Attack of M. Turgot in His Letter to Dr. Price* (2nd ed.) (Philadelphia: Budd & Bartram, 1797). Adams' work has been discussed at length in Charles A. Beard, *Economic Origins of Jeffersonian Democracy* (New York: The Free Press, 1915), at 299-321. Hereafter referred to as Beard, *Jeffersonian Democracy.*

and a tertium quid* *in the form of an independent executive holding for as long a term as possible should be introduced as a check on both the contending classes.*[4]

Expression of this theme of class conflict based on inequalities of material wealth can be found in virtually all eras of American history right up to the present. In Andrew Jackson's day, the dominant figure in the United States Senate, Thomas Hart Benton, stated in characteristically forceful language:

> *There never has been but two parties...founded in the radical question, whether PEOPLE, or PROPERTY, shall govern! Democracy implies a government by the people.... Aristocracy implies a government by the rich.... [A]nd in these words are contained the sum of party distinctions.*[5]

In the 1890's, Supreme Court Justice Henry B. Brown echoed the same sentiment:

> *The history of civilized society is largely a story of strife between those who have and those who have not.... [Social conflict arises from] the desire of the rich to obtain the labor of the poor at the lowest possible terms, the desire of the poor to obtain the uttermost farthing from the rich. The cause and the result of it all is the unequal distribution of property.*[6]

During the New Deal era, Robert H. Jackson, first Franklin D. Roosevelt's attorney general and later a Supreme Court Justice, stated:

> *Two kinds of power seem always in competition in*

---

* Some one thing acting as an intermediary between two other things.

4. Beard, *Jeffersonian Democracy*, at 316-17.

5. Quoted in Schlesinger, *The Age of Jackson*, at 125.

6. Quoted in Arnold M. Paul, *Conservative Crisis and the Rule of Law* (New York: Harper Torchbooks, 1960, at 85).

our democracy: there is political power, which is the
power of the voters, and there is economic power of
property, which is the power of its owners.[7]

The list of concurring viewpoints on this subject among politicians, historians, and political theorists could be extended almost indefinitely.

As suggested particularly by Benton and Jackson's statements, the wealthy and the needy are viewed by many theorists not only as competing factions whose interests must be reconciled but also as the two basic sources of political power in a representative democracy. Generally, candidates must attempt to accumulate decisive power through an alliance either with the wealthy, whose money is needed for effective media advertising, or with the masses, who can directly supply votes in very large numbers. And, in practice, American political parties have over the decades, despite their predisposition for playing both sides against the middle, for the most part conformed to this theory, with conservative parties (the Federalists, Whigs, and post-Lincoln Republicans) siding with the rich and their liberal counterparts (the Jeffersonian Republicans, Jacksonian Democrats, and modern Democrats) affiliating with the poor.

In short, the political and economic tension between the rich and the poor accounts for what is widely regarded as the most fundamental of all political issues. Since, under the United States system of government, political controversies tend sooner or later to become judicial controversies also, it is not surprising that this tension has repeatedly worked its way up to the Supreme Court in cases whose outcomes now form a major continuous thread of the institution's history.

After the fashion of political parties, Court Justices, too, have to varying degrees identified with the aspirations of either the wealthy or the needy. Any understanding of the Court's role in the clash of the classes, then, requires some delineation of the constellation of values, attitudes, and beliefs typically associated with the conservative and liberal viewpoints that have informed many Court opinions.

---

7. Robert H. Jackson, *The Struggle for Judicial Supremacy* (New York: Random House, 1941), at xii.

First, economic conservatism has typically been based on the conviction that no major attempts should be made by governments to redistribute wealth. Persons sympathetic with this outlook have classically contended that wealth is accessible to everyone who is willing to take advantage of natural opportunities. By this standard, the rich are considered to be fully entitled to savor the fruits of their superior abilities and effort, while poverty is seen as indicative of individual moral weakness.

To the economic conservative, the primary function of government in financial affairs should be to cultivate a favorable environment for the private pursuit of material well-being and to protect property owners against the recurring efforts of the poor to confiscate their holdings. At a minimum, government is expected to refrain from redistributing property and from interfering with its accumulation and enjoyment. Economic conservatives have traditionally also tended to regard the Supreme Court, and the judiciary in general, as an important buffer against the dangers of uncontrolled democracy as reflected in the popularly elected legislative and executive branches of government.

Taken together, these attributes describe an ideal economic conservative type that no single Supreme Court Justice has ever fully and consistently embodied. However, over the course of almost 200 years, numerous individuals whose influence on the Supreme Court has been important have embraced these values at least in substantial part. Among the most noteworthy are Alexander Hamilton, Chief Justice John Marshall, Justice Joseph Story, Justice Stephen J. Field, President and Chief Justice William Howard Taft, Justice James C. McReynolds, President Richard M. Nixon, and President Ronald Reagan.

Economic liberalism, on the other hand, is characterized by a belief that wealth should be distributed in such a way as to ease the burdens of poverty as much as possible. Here, wealth is seen neither as a sign of superior moral worth nor as a valid basis for license to do as one will even to the detriment of the public good. Similarly, poverty is viewed as an unfortunate result of hereditary and environmental processes rather than as evidence of inferior character. To the economic liberal, government's major function is to protect the poor from exploitation and, at a minimum, to refrain from granting special privileges to the rich.

As with conservatives, no single individual has ever fully and consistently embodied all the qualities that comprise an ideal economic liberal type. But liberal values have often found favor with Presidents and jurists who have left their mark on Supreme Court history. Among their ranks are President Thomas Jefferson, President Andrew Jackson, Chief Justice Roger B. Taney, Justice Samuel Freeman Miller, Justice Louis Dembitz Brandeis, President Franklin D. Roosevelt, and Justice William O. Douglas.

Caught up in ever shifting currents flowing between the opposing banks of economic conservatism and liberalism are political reform and counter-reform movements seeking to use legislatures and courts for the advantage of either the rich or the poor. After 200 years of fluctuating gains and losses on both sides, at least four themes have emerged out of these movements as recurrent in American history: (1) concerns over relief from excessive debts, (2) concerns over redistribution of wealth, (3) concerns over regulation of the behavior of the wealthy, and (4) concerns over support of organized action by the poor.

In keeping with these themes, regulatory laws have been enacted and social programs developed through the years to address each concern. Here are a few examples. For excessive debt: bankruptcy laws, stay laws (moratoria on debt foreclosure), and laws providing for currency inflation.[8] For redistribution of wealth: income tax, unemployment insurance, disability compensation, old age benefits, and other welfare programs. For regulation of the behavior of the wealthy: antitrust laws, maximum hour/minimum wage laws, child labor laws, laws prohibiting unfair business practices, laws regulating working conditions, and regulatory schemes based upon independent administrative agencies such as the Securities Exchange Commission and the Interstate Commerce Commission. For organized action by the poor: collective action measures pertaining to labor organizations, boycotts, and class actions.

---

8. Inflation of currency results in deflation of debts. As dollars become plentiful and less valuable, it becomes easier to pay off debts.

It is against the background of such very practical matters as these that the history of the United States Supreme Court has unfolded.

Chapter Two

The Constitution as
An Economic Document

During the years immediately preceding the birth of the United States, significant political tensions characterized the relationship between the New World's rich and its poor. The traditional political climate in colonial North America had been aristocratic and based largely upon the disenfranchisement of persons who did not own substantial property. But, as the revolutionary period amply demonstrated, populist sentiments concurrently enjoyed strong, widespread support.

The Revolutionary War brought about a shift in the existing power alignment between the haves and the have-nots. Many members of the propertied class were Tories who had remained loyal to England throughout the conflict. When the revolution succeeded, Tories were in many states deprived of political power and supplanted by leaders who based their politics on direct appeals to the masses rather than on the protection of vested wealth. The progressive leader Herbert Croly has summarized these historical events as follows:

> The Revolutionary War, while not exclusively the work of the popular element of the community, had undoubtedly increased considerably its power and influence. A large proportion of the well-to-do colonial Americans had been active or passive Tories, and had either been ruined or politically disorganized by the Revolution. Their successful opponents reorganized the state governments in a radical democratic spirit.

The power of the state was usually concentrated in the hands of a single assembly, to whom both the executive and the courts were subservient; and this method of organization was undoubtedly designed to give immediate and complete effect to the will of a popular majority.[9]

The post-war period from 1781 to 1789 in which the Articles of Confederation were in effect had a relatively populistic political climate. The federal government, at the time, lacked the power to tax and regulate commerce, and was therefore weak and ineffective. Real power lay in the hands of popularly elected state governments. These governments, responding to populist sentiments, enacted a number of statutes designed to aid the poor. For example, numerous bankruptcy statutes were passed allowing debtors to discharge their debts without full payment. Other legislative programs enacted to alleviate the burdens of the debtor class included stay laws, paper currency statutes designed to produce inflation, and laws abolishing debtors' prisons.[10] Such statutes caused grave alarm among the creditor class whose claims they jeopardized.

The populist movement during the period immediately preceding the Constitution had perhaps its most dramatic expression in Shays' Rebellion in 1786. A group of Massachusetts debtors led by Daniel Shays sought to obtain relief from hard times through a variety of measures including the issuance of paper money to inflate the currency and reduce the weight of their debts. When their efforts failed, Shays and his supporters engaged in armed revolt. Although the insurrection was quickly suppressed, it intensified the desire of the propertied class to create a government that could fully protect its interests.[11]

The convening of the 1787 Constitutional Convention in Philadelphia amounted to the beginning of a counterrevolution in which the propertied classes sought to regain power and create a government designed in large part to protect the vested interests of property holders against incursions by the masses.[12] The "Conclusions" reached at the end of Charles

---

9. Herbert Croly, *The Promise of American Life* (New York: E.P. Dutton & Co., 1963), at 31.

10. Beard, *Constitution*, at 28 & 31.

11. Leo Pfeffer, *This Honorable Court* (Boston: Beacon Press, 1965), at 35.

12. Beard, *Constitution, passim.*

Beard's *An Economic Interpretation of the Constitution of the United States* provide a vivid depiction of the attitudes of the creators and supporters of the Constitution with regard to the struggle between the rich and the poor:

> *The movement for the Constitution of the United States was originated and carried through principally by four groups of personalty [personal property] interests which had been adversely affected under the Articles of Confederation: money, public securities, manufactures, and trade and shipping....*
>
> *A large propertyless mass was, under the prevailing suffrage qualifications, excluded at the outset from participation (through representatives) in the work of framing the Constitution.*
>
> *The members of the Philadelphia Convention which drafted the Constitution were, with a few exceptions, immediately, directly and personally interested in, and derived economic advantages from the establishment of the new system.*
>
> *The Constitution was essentially an economic document based upon the concept that the fundamental private rights of property are anterior to government and morally beyond the reach of popular majorities.*
>
> *The major portion of the members of the Convention are on record as recognizing the claim of property to a special and defensive position in the Constitution.*[13]

As Madison explained on a number of occasions, the fundamental challenge facing the Constitutional Convention was the creation of a "democratic" government which would nevertheless provide full protection for the rights of the wealthy minority. This challenge was met by two different methods.

First, governmental power was so divided and fragmented as to make it extremely difficult for the majority to unite politically and impose its will on the minority. In this regard, a fundamental point to note is that the judicial branch was to be

---

13. *Id.* at 324-25.

a keystone in preventing democratic majorities from imposing their will on the wealthy minority. "[T]he crowning counterweight to an 'interested and overbearing majority,' as Madison phrased it, was secured in the peculiar position assigned to the judiciary, and the use of the sanctity and mystery of the law, as a foil to democratic attacks."[14]

Second, limits were placed on the power of state legislatures to enact statutes encroaching on the interests of the rich. The most important of these limits were the prohibitions upon the emission of paper money and upon the enactment of laws impairing the obligation of contracts.[15] As Alexander Hamilton put it, "The too frequent intermeddlings of the state legislatures in relation to private contracts were extensively felt and seriously lamented; and a Constitution which promised a preventative was, by those who felt and thought in this manner, eagerly embraced."[16]

The conflict over the ratification of the Constitution was extremely intense and divided along class lines with the holders of property favoring ratification and the debtor class opposing. As Beard states:

> No one can pore for weeks over the letters, newspapers and pamphlets of the years 1781-1789 without coming to the conclusion that there was a deep-coming conflict between a popular party based on paper money and agrarian interest, and a conservative party centered in the towns and resting on financial, mercantile, and personal property interests generally....[17]
>
> The opposition to the Constitution almost uniformly came from the agricultural regions, and from the areas in which debtors had been formulating paper money and other depreciatory schemes.[18]

Charles Warren, author of *The Supreme Court in United States History*, the most influential account to date of the

14. *Id.* at 161.
15. United States Constitution, art. I, sec. 10.
16. Letter of May 29, 1779 to George Washington, quoted in Beard, *Constitution*, at 180.
17. Beard, *Constitution*, at 292.
18. *Id.* at 291.

Court's history, has reached conclusions almost identical to those of Beard on this point. He has written:

> *Most of the opposition of the Anti-Federalists to the Constitution had been based on fears lest the proposed Federal Government should control the States in respect to their stay laws, their legal tender laws, their legislation as to British debts and loyalist properties and their State land grants and land titles.*[19]

A typical populist opponent of ratification was Luther Martin, a member of the Constitutional Convention who later opposed ratification on the ground that the Constitution prohibited state legislation on behalf of debtor and agrarian interests. Martin's views on the contract clause illustrate this position:

> *There might be times of great public calamities and distress, and of such extreme scarcity of specie, as should render it the duty of a government for the preservation of even the most valuable part of its citizens in some measure to interfere in their favor, by passing laws totally or partially stopping the courts of justice, or authorizing the debtor to pay by installments, or by delivering up his property to his creditors at a reasonable and honest valuation.*[20]

As the foregoing shows, the debate over the Constitution -both during the drafting and during the ratification process -was essentially a debate between defenders of property and defenders of the propertyless in which the latter were resoundingly defeated. It is perhaps fitting to conclude this discussion of the economic interests underlying the Constitution by quoting the conclusion (lengthy, but well worth careful attention) on this subject expounded by Chief Justice John Marshall in his *Life of George Washington*:

---

19. 1 Charles Warren, *The Supreme Court in United States History* (Boston: Little Brown & Co., 1922), at 62-63. Hereafter referred to as Warren, *The Supreme Court*.
20. Quoted in Beard, *Constitution*, at 205-206.

At length two great parties were formed in every state which were distinctly marked and which pursued distinct objects with systematic arrangement. The one struggled with unabated zeal for the exact observance of public and private engagements. By those belonging to it, the faith of a nation or of a private man was deemed a sacred pledge, the violation of which was equally forbidden by the principles of moral justice and of sound policy. The distresses of individuals were, they thought, to be alleviated only by industry and frugality, not by a relaxation of the laws or by a sacrifice of the rights of others. They were consequently the uniform friends of a regular administration of justice and of a vigorous course of taxation which would enable the state to comply with its engagements....

The other party marked out for themselves a more indulgent course. Viewing with extreme tenderness the case of the debtor, their efforts were unceasingly directed to his relief. To exact a faithful compliance with contracts was, in their opinion, a harsh measure which the people would not bear. They were uniformly in favor of relaxing the administration of justice, of affording facilities for the payment of debts, or of suspending their collection, and of remitting taxes. The same course of opinion led them to resist every attempt to transfer from their own hands into those of congress powers which by others were deemed essential to the preservation of the union. In many of these states, the party last mentioned constituted a decided majority of the people, and in all of them it was very powerful. The emission of paper money, the delay of legal proceedings, and the suspension of the collection of taxes were the fruits of their rule wherever they were completely predominant....

Throughout the union, a contest between these parties was periodically revived; and the public mind was perpetually agitated with hopes and fears on subjects which essentially affected the fortunes of a considerable portion of society.[21]

21. *Id.* at 297-299. This statement summarizes the main features of the eighteenth century variety of economic conservatism and liberalism.

Part Two

The First Conservative Era (1790-1835)

Chapter Three

The Washington Court (1790-1800)

During its first decade, the United States government was dominated by the Federalists, a political party composed primarily of the rich. As a leading scholar of the period has put it, "Surely the frankest politicians who ever graced the American scene, the Federalists made no pretense of being other than what they were: upper-class Americans who had a natural born right to rule their inferiors in the social and economic scale."[22] The nation's first President, George Washington, was a loyal Federalist, who selected his Federalist colleagues to fill essentially all the positions in the new government.

Although Washington was the nominal head of government, the dominant policy maker during the early 1790's was Alexander Hamilton, Washington's brilliant, energetic, and intensely conservative Secretary of the Treasury and author of the administration's major working papers. Hamilton was a strongly anti-democratic individual with an intense devotion to the protection and aggrandizement of the propertied classes and an equally intense distrust of the masses.

When Washington selected the six original members of the Supreme Court, he chose only Federalists who agreed generally with his and Hamilton's views regarding the purposes of the new government. The original Court, which opened for business in February 1790, was composed therefore of property holders who shared the same anti-democratic bias that characterized the Federalist movement.

---

22. John C. Miller, *The Federalist Era* (New York: Harper & Row, 1960), at 109.

Consider, for example, the first Chief Justice of the United States, John Jay (1790-95). The son of a wealthy merchant and husband of a member of the aristocratic Livingston family, Jay was a prominent lawyer who saw "the wise and the good" as locked in a never-ending struggle against "the wicked and the weak."[23] As one careful student of the Federalist era has commented, "[H]e was withal a conservative whose philosophy was succinctly expressed in the aphorism that 'those who own the country ought to govern it....' "[24] "[H]is entire career and his character made him anathema to the lower classes and their anti-Federalist leaders."[25]

The career of Justice James Wilson (1790-98) also vividly illustrates the economic conservatism of the Supreme Court in its earliest years. Wilson - "the Professor," as he was called at the time - was probably the "most democratic-minded" of the Court's charter members.[26] He was a successful Pennsylvania attorney, a leading member of the Constitutional Convention, and the co-author of the final draft of the Constitution. Although the most liberal of the original Justices, Wilson was the author of the constitutional clause asserting that "No State shall...pass any...Law impairing the Obligation of Contracts."[27] This so-called contract clause was to become the chief bastion of propertied interests during the pre-Jackson period of United States history. Wilson was heavily involved in land speculation and has been described as a "member and legal protector of the creditor class."[28] Obviously, this Court whose far left wing was occupied by James Wilson was a very conservative Court indeed.

The remaining four original Justices were kindred spirits to Jay and Wilson. John Rutledge (1790-91) had formerly served as South Carolina's governor. While holding that office, he had vetoed a proposed state constitution, on the ground that it was too democratic. He then resigned when the document was adopted over his veto.[29] William Cushing (1790-1810), the only

---

23. Pfeffer, *This Honorable Court*, at 37.
24. Miller, *The Federalist Era*, at 32.
25. Pfeffer, *This Honorable Court*, at 36.
26. *Id.* at 39.
27. United States Constitution, art. I, sec. 10.
28. Pfeffer, *This Honorable Court*, at 39.
29. Beard describes Rutledge as "one of the most ardent champions of the rights of property in government in the (Constitutional) Convention." Beard, *Constitution*, at 213.

Justice in the history of the Court to actually wear the traditional British judicial wig, presided over a number of Shays' Rebellion trials and there earned the rebels' hatred. John Blair (1790-96) was an independently wealthy Virginia attorney and a personal friend of Washington. James Iredell (1790-99) was a Federalist leader from North Carolina and one of the most ardent supporters of the Constitution from that state.[30]

Of the six, one commentator has noted:

> *These, then, were the first Supreme Court justices.... All were members or representatives of the propertied, creditor classes, and all believed that the purpose of government was to protect the rights of property against the covetous depredations of the lower classes.*[31]

Depicted in the form of a table, the distribution of the original six Justices was as follows:

TABLE A

Alignment of Justices - 1790

Liberal	Moderate	Conservative
	Wilson	Jay
		Rutledge
		Cushing
		Blair
		Iredell

For the remainder of the country's pre-Jeffersonian period (1790-1800), appointments to the Court did not appreciably alter the Bench's conservative character.[32] Indeed, if anything, they probably moved the Court even farther to the right. Rutledge's replacement, William Paterson (1793-1806), was a

---

30. Technically Iredell was not a charter member of the Court. Washington first appointed Robert H. Harrison, but Harrison resigned after five days and Iredell was appointed to replace him.

31. Pfeffer, *This Honorable Court*, at 41.

32. Appointments not mentioned in the text include Thomas Johnson (1792-93) and Alfred Moore (1800-04).

staunch Federalist and a member of the wealthy Van Rensselaer family. Blair's successor, Samuel Chase (1796-1811), was an arch-conservative who achieved the distinction of being "by far the most hated of the Federalist judges."[33] Chase's attitude on the rich-poor issue is strikingly illustrated by the following statement that he made to a grand jury:

> [T]he bulk of mankind are governed by their passions and not by reason.... The establishment of universal suffrage will take away all security for property and personal liberty...and our constitution will sink into a mobocracy, the worst of all popular governments.[34]

Oliver Ellsworth (1796-99), who replaced John Jay as Chief Justice, was an extremely wealthy right wing Federalist. As Beard has stated, "No member of the [Constitutional] Convention distrusted anything savoring of 'levelling democracy' more than Oliver Ellsworth."[35] Bushrod Washington (1799-1829), who filled the chair vacated by the more moderate Wilson, was the President's nephew. Over the years, he provided a proxy vote for John Marshall (1801-35), "the last of the Federalists," who was to later transform the Federalist credo of economic conservatism from a political platform into a set of legal principles that dominated the American legal system for decades.

As two early rulings illustrate, the Washington Court wasted little time in applying its principles of economic conservatism to the law. In 1791, for one, Rhode Island passed a statute granting a debtor a three year extension on the payment of his debts and exempted him from arrest and attachment during that period. Chief Justice Jay and Justice Cushing, on circuit, held the Rhode Island statute unconstitutional under Justice Wilson's contract clause stating, "[T]he Legislature of a State have no right to make a law to exempt an individual from arrests and his estate from attachments for his private debts, for any term of time, it being clearly a law impairing the obliga-

---

33. Pfeffer, *This Honorable Court*, at 86.
34. 1 Warren, *The Supreme Court*, at 277.
35. Beard, *Constitution*, at 196.

tion of contracts, and therefore contrary to the Constitution of the United States."[36]

Perhaps the best illustration of an economically conservative decision handed down by the Washington Court, sitting *en banc* rather than on circuit, can be found in *Ware v. Hylton* (1796).[37] An issue that caused intense political excitement among the American debtor class at the time concerned the payment of debts owed to the British. In Virginia alone, it has been estimated that such debts amounted to more than $2,000,000. Various states enacted laws rescinding these debts or allowing payment in depreciated currency. When the matter came before the Supreme Court, the Bench held that the state laws were contrary to applicable treaty provisions and that the British debts must be paid in full.

The Supreme Court did not, however, play a major role in thwarting economic reform during the 1790's. In its first decade of existence, the Court was a very weak branch of government. During its first five years, the Bench had almost no business at all, since time was required for cases to work their way up through the new federal court system. Most of the Justices' days were spent in circuit riding. When they did sit together, they functioned more as an admiralty court than as a third major branch of government.

The Court's early weakness also stemmed in large part from the fact that the Constitution did not provide an explicit definition of the Bench's powers, so the Court was left to build up its authority gradually over the years. Not until 1819 did the Court attempt to exercise real political power in opposition to other branches of government.

---

36. Champion v. Casey (unreported), discussed in 1 Warren, *The Supreme Court*, at 66-68.
37. 3 U.S. (3 Dall.) 199 (1796), discussed in 1 Warren, *The Supreme Court*, at 144-46.

Chapter Four

The Court in the Shadow of Jefferson (1801-1812)[38]

1801 was a milestone in Supreme Court history because it marked the arrival of the "Great Chief Justice," John Marshall (1801-1835). If a vote were taken among lawyers and judges to choose the most important person in the history of the American judiciary, Marshall would no doubt win by a large margin. More than any other individual, he laid the foundation of the American legal system, a foundation that still stands in large part today. Modest, sloppy in appearance, woefully lacking in formal legal education, unfailingly genial, Marshall proved irresistably persuasive to most of his colleagues on the Court that he dominated for a third of a century. "The last Federalist," he pursued his pet values of nationalism and economic conservatism with dogged consistency and astonishing success.

Ironically, 1801 also marked the inauguration of Marshall's cousin and most formidable antagonist, President Thomas Jefferson, who cast a shadow across Supreme Court history that eclipsed Marshall's light for at least a decade. Jefferson, the "man of the people," had a nearly lifelong hatred for Marshall and the aristocratic values for which Marshall stood. Jefferson proved to be the only adversary, with the possible exception of Andrew Jackson, who could hold Marshall at bay. The period of Supreme Court history from 1801 to roughly 1812 can perhaps best be understood in terms of the struggle between Marshall's Federalist majority on the Court and Jefferson's anti-Federalist forces in the executive and legislative branches, a struggle in which Jefferson, for the most part, prevailed.

---

38. The principal sources of material presented in this chapter are Beard, *Jeffersonian Democracy*; and 1 Warren, *The Supreme Court in United States History*, at 170-399.

While conservative entrenchment on the first Supreme Court was undisputably secured by the Federalists, concurrently, in another arena, their honeymoon was ending. In the early 1790's, Jefferson broke ranks with the conservatives who, under Hamilton's leadership, had dominated the Washington administration and converted the federal government into a special preserve of Federalist property owners. After resigning from his position as Washington's Secretary of State, Jefferson began to gather the political support of people who felt the national government should cease its practice of granting special favors to industrial and mercantile interests. According to Beard, "Hamilton's economic policies were the fundamental source of the party cleavage."[39] Beard continued:

> *Thousands of small farmers and debtors and laboring mechanics were opposed to his [Hamilton's] policies, but they did not have the organization or consciousness of identity of interests which was necessary to give them weight in the councils of the new government. They were partly disenfranchised under the existing laws, and they had no leaders worthy of mention.... It required the astute leadership of Jefferson, and the creation of a federal machine under his direction, to consolidate the heterogeneous petty interests against the Federalist group.*[40]

When Hamilton refused to make adequate concessions to the burgeoning democratic sentiments of the 1790's, even the Federalists split into a conservative wing under the leadership of Hamilton and a moderate wing under the leadership of John Adams. The growing strength of the anti-Federalist forces was vividly demonstrated by the presidential election of 1796, in which the moderate Federalist Adams eked out a razor-thin victory over Jefferson with an electoral college margin of three.

The anti-Federalist movement came to a head in the 1800 election, in which Jefferson defeated Adams. The significance of this election has been described as follows: "The Presiden-

---

39. Beard, *Jeffersonian Democracy*, at 112.
40. Beard, *Constitution*, at 103.

tial election of 1800 marks a turning point in our national history no less important than does the adoption of our present Constitution. It signalized the initial victory of the first political party which professed to represent the American people."[41]

The fact that economic issues were of fundamental concern in the contest is demonstrated by the intense, almost apocalyptic anxiety felt by the wealthy industrial and mercantile community regarding Jefferson's election. As "Decius" wrote in the *Columbian Centinel*: "Tremble then in case of Jefferson's election, all ye holders of public lands, for your ruin is at hand."[42]

What was it about Jefferson's political and economic views that made them seem so revolutionary and dangerous to the leaders of finance and industry? One way to answer this question is to summarize the views of the intellectual godfather of Jeffersonian democracy, John Taylor, the Virginia farmer and political theorist who articulated the core principles of Jeffersonianism in perhaps their most ideal form.[43] Taylor's analysis, like that of Madison and Adams, focused sharply on the economic issue of unequal distribution of wealth. Taylor, however, in contrast to Adams and Hamilton, denied that inequality is inevitable. As Beard has written:

At the outset of his plea for a republic based upon substantial equality, Taylor is compelled to face Adams' fundamental proposition that such a system of government is impossible because the sources of inequality 'are founded in the constitution of nature,' and cannot be eradicated no matter what institutional devices are invented.... He [Taylor] simply denies its validity.[44]

---

41. Professor O.G. Libby as quoted in Beard, *Jeffersonian Democracy*, at 15.

42. *Columbian Centinal*, August 27, 1800, quoted in Beard, *Jeffersonian Democracy*, at 360.

43. Taylor is often referred to as "John Taylor of Caroline." The main source of this exposition of his ideas is Beard, *Jeffersonian Democracy*, at 322-352. Jefferson "thoroughly indorsed Taylor's *Inquiry into the Principles and Policy of the Government of the United States*...and declared that Col. Taylor and he had never differed on any political principle of importance." Beard, *Jeffersonian Democracy*, at 415 n.l.

44. *Id.* at 323.

In Taylor's view, inequality is the result of exploitation, not of superior virtue:

> He [Taylor] will not admit that the great differences in wealth, the abysmal division into rich and poor, are historically the product of the industry of the few and the sloth of the many. On the contrary, he holds that the older aristocracies...were begotten...by exploitation, not by thrift and savings.[45]

The specifically American form of aristocracy, according to Taylor, was based upon wealth achieved through manipulation of the financial system (stocks, bonds, currency, etc.). The remedy against exploitation by the financial oligarchy, he proposed, was to use the political process to destroy this class's special privileges.

Thomas Jefferson's politics were based on essentially the same principles as Taylor's. Jefferson shared Taylor's hostility toward merchants and financiers who were the leaders of Hamiltonian capitalism, and he made his political appeal to the masses of small farmers who comprised the most populous element of society.[46] To quote Beard once again:

> Jefferson's views on fundamental economic questions were not matters of speculation. In his Notes on Virginia he had denounced the arts of the merchant and the financier, and declared the landowning farmer to be the only hope of a republic. He had made it plain that the methods of capitalism were not only highly objectionable to him personally, but that, in his opinion, an extensive development of them was incompatible with the perpetuity of American institutions.[47]

---

45. Id.
46. Jefferson's politics were not simply a matter of rich versus poor. His respect for the small farmer did not extend to the urban artisan. Thus, for Jefferson, the fundamental issue was the farmer against the city dweller, rather than the poor against the rich. Nevertheless, since the small farmers were mostly impoverished, the rich-poor issue was always implicitly present.
47. Beard, *Jeffersonian Democracy*, at 358.

Jefferson's political platform, however, was not based upon the concept of a powerful national government acting vigorously on behalf of the small farmer. His program was simply to stop the national government from granting special privileges to the capitalist class and to return to a basically laissez faire system.

In this regard, it is important to recognize that, over the course of American history, economic conservatives and liberals have exactly reversed themselves with regard to the desirability of strong government intervention in economic affairs. During the nation's early years, conservatives such as Hamilton and Marshall favored a strong, active national government. Since, at the time, government was dominated by the wealthy, a strong government was then normally one that vigorously aided property owners. Concurrently, liberals such as Jefferson endorsed a laissez faire role for government in which special privileges were not granted to the wealthy. As the franchise spread and the ballot became a vehicle of political power for the masses, Andrew Jackson, Franklin D. Roosevelt and other liberals favored strong government action on behalf of the poor, and conservatives such as Stephen J. Field, Richard Nixon, and Ronald Reagan came to support a policy of reducing regulation of the economy, particularly where benefits to the poor had accrued.

After their defeat in the 1800 election, the Federalists turned their hopes to the judiciary as the branch of government that might continue to carry out Federalist policies. One of President Adams' last important acts was to appoint John Marshall as Chief Justice and standard-bearer for the Federalist forces in the judiciary. When Jefferson took office in March 1801, essentially all the judges in the federal court system were still Federalists, and, since they were appointed for life, years would pass before the anti-Federalist faction could take over.

Jefferson himself fully understood this situation and wrote, "[T]he Federalists have retired into the Judiciary as a stronghold...and from that battery all the works of republicanism are to be beaten down and erased."[48] As it was to turn out, he never succeeded in breaking the Federalist hold on the judicial system.

When Jefferson was inaugurated, the conservatives com-

---

48. Quoted in 1 Warren, *The Supreme Court*, at 193.

pletely controlled the Supreme Court. Chief Justice John Marshall was a consistent economic conservative. For Marshall, the Court's duty to protect the rich was second in importance only to its duty to enhance the power of the Court and the federal government. Marshall's economic conservatism was fully supported by the Court's remaining five members. Bushrod Washington was a conservative Federalist who allied himself closely with Marshall.[49] Chase, as we have seen, was for the most part a right-wing reactionary. And the remaining three Justices, Cushing, Paterson, and Moore, were also staunch Federalists. In short, upon assuming the Presidency, Jefferson was confronted by a Supreme Court with a solid 6-0 conservative majority.

Despite the efforts of three successive Republican Presidents, Jefferson, Madison, and James Monroe, to change the situation, this dominance was not definitively broken until Marshall's death in 1835. Several factors combined to thwart the Republican efforts to liberalize the Bench. First, Jefferson, Madison, and Monroe made only six appointments to the Court during their combined 24 years in office.[50] Marshall and Washington survived into the Jackson era. With the Court manned by only six Justices up to 1807 and seven thereafter,[51] the two needed only an additional pair of sympathizers among the remaining Justices in order to control the Court. And the Republican appointments gave them exactly what they needed.

From the perspective of anti-Federalist politics, Jefferson, Madison, and Monroe did not choose their Justices wisely. Only William Johnson (1804-34) was able to make a decent show-

---

49. Toward the end of his long career on the Court, Washington showed some tendencies to move away from Marshall's hard-line economic conservatism. *See, e.g.,* Ogden v. Sanders, 25 U.S. (12 Wheat.) 213 (1827). During the 1801-12 period, however, Washington was a reliable member of the conservative bloc.

50. Jefferson appointed William Johnson (1804-34), H. Brockholst Livingston (1806-23), and Thomas Todd (1807-26). Madison appointed Joseph Story (1812-45) and Gabriel Duval (1812-35). Monroe appointed Smith Thompson (1824-43). During the 12 years from 1812 to 1823, no appointments to the Supreme Court were made. This remains the longest period without appointments in Supreme Court history to date.

51. The seventh seat was created by Congressional enactment in 1807.

52. For a detailed discussion of Justice Johnson, see Donald G. Morgan, *Justice William Johnson, The First Dissenter* (Columbia, South Carolina: University of South Carolina Press, 1954). Hereafter referred to as Morgan, *Justice William Johnson.* Johnson was the first Justice in United States Supreme Court history who had substantial tendencies toward economic liberalism. Although by no means radical, Johnson was much more inclined than the other Justices to grant federal and state legislatures broad power to legislate

ing on behalf of Jeffersonian concepts.[52] Both Henry Livingston (1807-23), a political and economic moderate, and Thomas Todd (1807-26), a Kentucky land lawyer, "promptly disappeared into the shadow of Marshall."[53] Maryland aristocrat Gabriel Duval (1812-35) was also a reliable Marshall supporter.[54] And Joseph Story (1812-45), with whom we shall become more familiar in subsequent chapters, turned out to be an arch-conservative who provided another vote for the Marshall-Washington bloc.[55] Story's role on the Supreme Court has been described as follows:

> *Story was quickly and completely captured by (or, perhaps more accurately, surrendered to) Marshall. The relationship between them was somewhat like that between Boswell and Samuel Johnson, one not merely of deep affection but of hero worship.*[56]

The following table illustrates the conservative dominance on the Court after Jefferson's three appointees had been seated:

TABLE B

Alignment of Justices - 1807 to 1812

Liberal	Moderate	Conservative
	Johnson	Marshall
	Livingston	Washington
		Chase
		Cushing
		Todd

---

in the public interest at the expense of vested property rights. "From the outset, the young Jeffersonian judge (Johnson) had looked with deference upon the rights of property.... But Johnson found that the public, too, had important interests in the law.... Provided its voice was clear and unequivocal, the national legislature might pass 'severe laws' in protecting the public interest." *Id.* at 208.

53. Pfeffer, *This Honorable Court*, at 93.

54. For further discussion of Duval and his role on the Court, see p. 42 *infra*.

55. Story was nominally a Republican, but he was a conservative through and through in his political and judicial beliefs. At the time of his appointment, former President Jefferson warned President Madison that Story was a "pseudo-Republican" and not to be trusted. 1 Warren, *The Supreme Court*, at 417.

56. Pfeffer, *This Honorable Court*, at 41.

A second factor contributing to the continued Federalist control of the Court was the unusual degree of dominance exercised by Chief Justice Marshall. Jefferson wrote, "It will be difficult to find a character of firmness enough to preserve his independence on the same bench with Marshall."[57] As it happened, only Johnson met this specification, and he was simply overmatched by the Marshall-Washington wing of the Court.

Finally, the failure of the anti-Federalists to capture the Court was partially the result of the failure of the Republican Party to generate a viable political program.[58] Once in power, the forces of Jeffersonian democracy turned out to be far from the radicals that the Federalists had feared in 1800. Jefferson himself moved rapidly back toward the political center after his inauguration and was later followed there by Madison and Monroe. By the time Monroe took office, the Republicans had adopted many of the views of the old Federalists.

Given a series of surprisingly conservative apppointments, Marshall's strengths, and the lack of a viable Republican political program, how then was Jefferson, at least, able to hold the Supreme Court at bay?

The answer is that the dominant forces of Jeffersonianism were able to mount a sharp and effective attack on the Court. First, the Justices, for all practical purposes, were put out of business for 14 months during 1802 and 1803 by legislation which was ostensibly designed merely to change the dates of the Court's Terms, but which was really intended to give the Court an involuntary "vacation." Second, an attempted impeachment of Justice Chase fell only four votes shy of success. Third, repeated efforts were made in Congress to enact legislation and constitutional amendments stripping the Court of its power. These events intimidated even Marshall, as is demonstrated by the following astonishing statement made by him in a letter to Chase:

I think the modern doctrine of impeachment should yield to an appellate jurisdiction in the legislature. A

---

57. *Id.* at 93.
58. This failure was basically the result of the anachronistic qualities of the Jeffersonian political credo. Given the irresistible drive toward industrial development, it was simply not possible to maintain political power with an imagery and a political program based upon notions of an agrarian arcadia.

reversal of those legal opinions deemed unsound by the legislature would certainly better comport with the mildness of our character than a removal of the judge who had rendered them unknowing of his fault.[59]

As a result, it has been said that "Marshall's contribution to the evolution of the Court may lie as much in the decisions that he did not make as in those that he did.... Marshall was too prudent to present Jefferson and the Republicans with an all-out challenge at the height of their popularity and at the nadir of the Federalists."[60]

Accordingly, it can safely be concluded that the inability of Jefferson to capture the Court did not make any great impact until after Jefferson left office. The Court did not, during Jefferson's tenure, impose any major obstacles to economic reforms.[61] Instead, it stood passively aside as the Jefferson administration cut military spending, discontinued the production of war vessels, repealed the lucrative positions of the midnight judges created at the last minute by the Adams administration,[62] abolished excise taxes on whiskey, reduced the public debt, and carried out numerous other measures to weaken "the right to use Government for the benefit of any capitalistic groups, fiscal, banking, or manufacturing."[63]

After Jefferson's 1809 departure from the presidency, the Supreme Court began gradually to take an activist role in support of economic conservatism, a trend whose emergence became vividly apparent in the ruling handed down in *Fletcher*

---

59. Quoted in Pfeffer, *This Honorable Court*, at 87.

60. Pfeffer, *This Honorable Court*, at 78.

61. Of course, the most famous case of all, Marbury v. Madison, 5 U.S. (1 Cranch 137 (1803), was decided during this period. As repeatedly pointed out by commentators, however, the genius of the *Marbury* case was its assertion of the great principles of judicial review and governmental accountability to the rule of the law in a context which did not require an order that Jefferson and his colleagues could disobey. The Court did not, during Jefferson's tenure, take an activist role in the formulation of political and economic policy. As Pfeffer has stated, "The only major decision that Marshall issued during the eight years Jefferson was President was *Marbury*." *This Honorable Court*, at 95.

62. The repeal of Adams' midnight judges act was challenged in litigation that reached the Supreme Court. In Stuart v. Laird, 5 U.S. (1 Cranch) 299 (1803), Marshall upheld the constitutionality of the repealing statute. The case provides a good symbol of Marshall's passivity during the period when the Court was under the shadow of Jefferson.

63. Beard, *Jeffersonian Democracy*, at 467. For a general discussion of the economic policies of the Jefferson administration, *see id.* at 435-67.

v. Peck (1810)[64]. This case, which has been discussed at length by many commentators, involved the famous Yazoo land grants made by the Georgia legislature. In all, 35 million acres of land in the present states of Alabama and Mississippi were granted to syndicates of private investors at a bargain price. Thereafter the existence of wholesale bribery of Georgia legislators who voted for the grants came to light.

A subsequent Georgia legislature passed a statute rescinding the grants. The speculators brought suit challenging the constitutionality of the rescinding legislation and the litigation was carried to the Supreme Court. Although some small investors were involved, the case presented a classic rich-poor issue. It set syndicates of wealthy investors, largely from New England, against the people of Georgia. The Court ruled that the rescinding legislation was a law impairing the obligation of contracts and hence void. The speculators kept their lands. More important, the contract clause was converted into the Court's most powerful weapon in its battle against economic reform efforts by state legislatures.

Fletcher v. Peck vividly illustrates the economic conservatism of the Court of 1810 and indicates that Marshall and his Associates were finally ready to move out from under Jefferson's shadow and to assert their policies of nationalism and economic conservatism in an activist manner. Nevertheless, the case was an exception to the general pattern of judicial restraint that characterized the 1801-1812 period, a pattern summarized by Supreme Court historian and Harvard Professor Robert J. McCloskey as follows: "[T]he Court after 1810 was for some time no more formidable than it had been before.... Marshall was holding back, awaiting a more propitious future."[65]

---

64. 10 U.S. (6 Cranch) 87 (1810).
65. Robert G. McCloskey, *The American Supreme Court* (Chicago: The University of Chicago Press, 1960) at 40.

Chapter 5

The Prime and Decline of the Marshall Court (1812-1835)[66]

Defeated in the open field by Jefferson, Federalism had retreated to prepared defenses. Under the resourceful leadership of John Marshall it entrenched itself in the courts of law and sought to make them unshakable bulwarks against change.[67]

In 1812, Supreme Court history took an ironic turn. Justice Cushing had died in 1810, and Justice Chase in 1811. After an exasperating delay of nearly 12 years, the Jeffersonians had the chance to obtain a majority on the Court. "[O]ld Cushing is dead," wrote Jefferson at the time, "At length, then, we have a chance of getting a Republican majority in the Supreme Judiciary."[68] Yet the Court that emerged after the appointments of 1812 was nearly as conservative as the Federalist Courts of the 1790's. Why?

From the liberals' perspective, Madison committed the equivalent of a chess player's queen sacrifice in selecting replacements for Cushing and Chase. The alignment on the Court as late as 1810 was five economic conservatives (Marshall, Washington, Chase, Cushing, and Todd) and two moderates (Johnson and Livingston). The deaths of Cushing and Chase reduced the conservative wing to three. If economic progressives had been appointed to fill the vacant slots, the liberals and moderates would have enjoyed a 4-3 majority.

---

66. Marshall, of course, had been Chief Justice since 1801, but it was not until roughly 1812 that the forces of economic conservatism recovered sufficiently from the Jeffersonian boom to reestablish their confidence and begin to move boldly.

67. Schlesinger, *The Age of Jackson*, at 322.

68. Quoted in 1 Warren, *The Supreme Court*, at 403.

Instead, Madison appointed two more conservatives, Joseph Story and Gabriel Duval. The reason remains a mystery.[69] In Story's case, perhaps Madison was simply tired; his first three nominations for the spot had failed to receive Senate approval. In any case, the outcome is not a mystery: Marshall's conservative wing retained control.

Story, as has been mentioned, was an arch-conservative who rapidly became John Marshall's strongest admirer.[70] And Duval was also a generally conservative Justice who rarely disagreed with Marshall.[71] As a result, the Court that emerged in 1812 and remain unchanged until 1823 was, once again, composed of a solid five-vote conservative bloc and only two moderates.

TABLE C

Alignment of Justices - 1812-1823

Liberal	Moderate	Conservative
	Johnson	Marshall
	Livingston	Story
		Washington
		Todd
		Duval

The economic conservatism of this Court is not subject to serious dispute. As Justice Johnson's biographer was to write of

---

69. *Id.* at 415.

70. 1 Leon Friedman & Fred L. Israel, *The Justices of the United States* (New York: Chelsea House, 1969), at 435-53. Story's was "a conservatism in which property and contract became the central institutions from which all other values prescinded." *Id.* at 440. At the Massachusetts constitutional convention of 1820, for example, Story "was outspoken in his defense of vested rights and pleaded for virtual disenfranchisement of the urban working classs." *Id.* at 446. According to Story, the main problem of government was "how the property-holding part of the community may be sustained against the inroads of poverty and vice." Quoted in Schlesinger, *The Age of Jackson*, at 269. Story was "highly obnoxious to Jefferson," who, in turn, referred to him as a "pseudo-Republican" and "unquestionably a tory." 1 Warren, *The Supreme Court*, at 406.

71. "Justice Duval generally supported Chief Justice Marshall's constitutional views." 1 Friedman & Israel, *The Justices of the United States*, at 419. Indeed, Duval disagreed with Marshall in only one significant constitutional case, Dartmouth College v. Woodward, 17 U.S. (4 Wheat.) 518 (1819). So complete was Duval's acquiescence that he filed only one dissenting opinion in his 22 years on the Court! Duval's conservatism is not surprising since he was a member of one of the wealthiest and most important landholding families in Maryland.

it, "The Court of John Marshall has acquired a reputation for extreme solicitude for vested rights. Its steady effort to shield from government interference the interests of property holders has become a byword to historians."[72]

1812 presented Marshall with much more than just the simple assurance of a continued conservative majority on the Supreme Court. At the time, the "propitious future" he awaited appeared to be dawning concurrently with a major shift in the nation's economic and political life. This midway point through the tenure of the Republican presidential trio of Jefferson, Madison, and Monroe is perhaps, then, as good a chronological point as any from which to demarcate the beginning of "the prime of the Marshall Court."[73]

The War of 1812 provided a substantial boost to the youthful capitalistic system that had been nurtured by Hamilton. The burst of industrial development that accompanied the war emphasized a point that was becoming increasingly apparent to all: the agrarian arcadia of Jefferson's dreams was simply not going to be. America's future was to be one of industrial revolution and growth.

In addition, the voices of Henry Clay and Daniel Webster, the leading spokesmen of mid-century conservatism, were becoming stronger in the nation's councils. They espoused an "American system," an economic order based upon indigenous industry, financed by a vigorous national bank, and nurtured by protective tariffs. During their respective presidencies, Madison and Monroe could feel the wind changing and shifted increasingly toward political postures surprisingly akin to those of the old-time Federalists.

Few issues of major economic importance reached the Supreme Court until 1819. In that year, the nation experienced a major financial panic and the beginnings of a severe depression that was to last almost a decade. Depressions normally lead to demands for economic reform and this one was no exception. In three important cases decided in 1819, however, the

---

72. Morgan, *Justice William Johnson*, at 207.

73. A case can be made, however, that the Marshall Court's activism began earlier. As we have seen, the Court in 1810 had used the contract clause and the notion of vested property rights to declare unconstitutional the efforts of the Georgia legislature to recapture the fraudulent profits gained by land speculators in the infamous Yazoo land transactions. Fletcher v. Peck, 10 U.S. (6 Cranch) 87 (1810).

Marshall Court made dramatic moves to contain the burgeoning economic reform movement and to prevent it from impinging upon the interests of the rich.

The first was *Sturges v. Crowninshield*, [74] a famous case that has been much discussed by commentators and that dramatically illustrates Marshall's unwillingness to allow relief legislation to harm the interests of the creditor class. Because of Congress' failure to exercise its authority to enact a national bankruptcy act,[75] a number of states moved to protect their debtors by passing their own. In *Sturges*, a New York bankruptcy law was held unconstitutional as applied to contracts executed prior to the measure's approval. Speaking for the Court, Marshall concluded that the New York statute violated the constitutional provision prohibiting states from enacting legislation "impairing the Obligations of Contracts."[76] Moreover, his opinion suggested that all state bankruptcy laws, if challenged before the Bench, would similarly be held unconstitutional, including those applying to contracts executed after their passage.[77] This amounted to a bold attack on one of the most central and recurrent economic reform demands, namely statutes allowing debtors, in hard times, to deviate from the terms of their contracts. As in *Fletcher v. Peck*, Marshall had again "exalted the constitutional contract clause as a barrier against relief legislation."[78]

The second landmark decision of 1819 was *McCulloch v. Maryland*.[79] In this matter, Marshall gave urgently needed shelter to the Bank of the United States, a financial institution that was the central pillar in the entire Hamiltonian scheme of government-protected industry. This "hated banking corporation"[80] had lapsed in 1811, having become "an object of general odium, due partly to the fact that it was under almost complete

---

74. 17 U.S. (4 Wheat.) 120 (1819).

75. United States Constitution, art. I, sec. 8 states, "The Congress shall have Power...to establish...uniform Laws on the subject of Bankruptcies throughout the United States...."

76. As stated in the text accompanying note 27 *supra*, the contract clause provides "No State shall...pass any...Law impairing the Obligation of Contracts...." United States Constitution, art. I, sec. 10.

77. This dictum was later repudiated, over Marshall's dissent, in Ogden v. Sanders, 25 U.S. (12 Wheat.) 135 (1927), discussed below.

78. Morgan, *Justice William Johnson*, at 117.

79. 17 U.S. (4 Wheat.) 316 (1819).

80. 1 Warren, *The Supreme Court*, at 504.

control of the Federalists...."[81] Over intense opposition, the bank was rechartered in 1816 during the nationalistic euphoria of the era of good feelings. "Within two years, however, by reason of bad management and mistaken policies, which had first encouraged over-expansion of credits and later drastically curtailed them, thereby ruining many State banks, the Bank had brought upon itself the intense hatred of the whole South and West."[82]

When the terrible crash of 1819 occurred, "the general public placed the responsibility on that 'monster', the Bank of the United States."[83] Legislation designed to break the Bank's power was passed in numerous states, including a heavy Maryland tax on all notes issued by the Bank within that state. Litigation concerning the Maryland tax was carried to the Supreme Court, where Marshall, adopting the arguments of the Bank's celebrated attorneys, Daniel Webster, William Pinckney, and William Wirt, held the tax unconstitutional.

The most important aspect of Marshall's opinion was his broad reading of the Constitution's "necessary and proper" clause[84] to confer upon Congress broad discretion to select whatever means are convenient for exercising its delegated powers. Although the power to create a bank is not explicitly mentioned in the Constitution, Marshall held that it is implied since Congress might rationally believe that the use of a corporation is convenient for carrying out its fiscal power. Having found that Congress had the power to charter a bank, Marshall proceeded to hold that the constitutional clause establishing that "[T]he laws of the United States...shall be the supreme Law of the Land...."[85] bans the states from taxing the Bank of the United States.

The *McCulloch* opinion was vintage Marshall. In a single stroke, he succeeded in vastly augmenting the power of the national government and in protecting the powerful pro-Bank interests. The response of the Jeffersonians was outrage. Jefferson, Madison, and Spencer Roane, Virginia's ardently Republican Chief Justice, were furious. The *Niles Register*, a

---

81. *Id.*
82. *Id* at. 505.
83. *Id.*
84. United States Constitution, art. I, sec. 8.
85. United States Constitution, art. VI.

leading Republican newspaper, called the case a "judicial decision which threatens to annihilate the sovereignties of the States...and make the productive many subservient to the unproductive few...."[86]

The third "great case" of 1819 was *Dartmouth College v. Woodward*,[87] which again used the contract clause to strike down reform efforts by the Republicans.[88] Frustrated by the policies of the Federalist-dominated board of directors of Dartmouth College, the New Hampshire Republican Party attempted to modify the college's charter to make the college more responsive to current attitudes. Marshall thwarted this effort by holding, for the first time, that corporate charters are contracts within the meaning of the contract clause and that states therefore cannot enact laws impairing the obligations set forth in corporate charters. The case was a clear victory for vested rights. Morever, it laid down a doctrine of extremely far-reaching potential for protecting the corporations which were to become the basic organizational units of the American industrial system.

The Jeffersonians, naturally enough, were deeply angered by the 1819 trilogy of conservative-activist rulings. Jefferson himself, no less than the others, shared in the dismay. In 1820, he wrote, "The Judiciary of the United States is the subtle corps of sappers and miners constantly working underground to undermine the foundations of our confederated fabric."[89] In 1821, he wrote to Roane, "The great object of my fear is the Federal Judiciary. That body...is ingulphing insidiously the special governments into the jaws of that which feeds them.... Let the eye of vigilance never be closed."[90]

This 1819 trilogy of Supreme Court rulings was no doubt one of the most dramatic developments in the entire history of the Court's involvement in rich-poor controversies. Above everything else, it marked the first major instance of vigorous conservative judicial activism. Previously, the Federalist Justices had played a rather passive role in deciding the

---

86. 1 Warren, *The Supreme Court*, at 523.

87. 17 U.S. (4 Wheat.) 518 (1819).

88. Both the *McCulloch* and *Dartmouth College* cases were argued by Daniel Webster, one of the most successful and eloquent defenders of property rights in the history of the United States.

89. 1 Warren, *The Supreme Court*, at 546.

90. *Id.* at 546-47.

economic disputes brought before them. Now, a decisive intent to intervene in the nation's political processes on behalf of the rich was revealed. Moreover, in a single Term, the Marshall Court managed both (1) to limit the power of the states to enact legislation on behalf of the poor and (2) to expand the power of the federal government to enact legislation on behalf of the great financial powers of the nation. Evidently Marshall hoped that, as precedent, *Sturges, McCulloch,* and *Dartmouth College* would provide useful weapons in the struggle to secure the rights of property against reform efforts by the masses.[91]

1819 marked the apex in Marshall's career as a champion of property rights. That year's depression extended deep into the 1820's, troubling the last term of James Monroe, making the presidency of John Quincy Adams an agony for him, and leading at last to Andrew Jackson's 1828 election. The persistent hard times and the increased demands for reform and relief took their toll on political and popular tolerance for Marshall and the rich. This period has been described by Arthur Schlesinger Jr., author of *The Age of Jackson,* as follows:

> *The eighteen-twenties were a decade of discontent, born in depression, streaked with suffering and panic, shaken by bursts of violence and threats of rebellion. Jefferson's despondency, the intricate anxieties of John Taylor of Caroline, the furious despair of John Randolph, reflected this unrest in the moods of weary elder statesmen. But its main source was the profound frustration of thriving and vigorous classes who felt the central government to be hostile to their needs and interest. The planters of the South, the workingmen of the North, those small farmers of the North and West unconvinced by Henry Clay, could not but have grave misgivings over the workings of the American system. It seemed to them, as it was belatedly seeming to Jefferson, a betrayal of the Jeffersonian promise of equal rights in favor of special benefits for a single class....*

---

91. The Marshall Court's activism on behalf of the rich did not by any means end with the year 1819. *See* Green v. Biddle, 21 U.S. (8 Wheat.) 1 (1823), which struck down a Kentucky law providing that absentee owners could not evict settlers from their land without compensation to the settlers for improvements made to the land, and Craig v. Missouri, 29 U.S. (4 Pet.) 410 (1830), which held that "loan-certificates" issued by the state of Missouri, to combat financial distress and panic, were illegal "bills of credit."

> Under strong popular pressure many of the states passed 'relief' legislation, in the form of stop laws, stays of execution, and the establishment of state banks licensed to issue millions in paper. 'Relief', of course, simply produced further inflation, bringing back those happy times when 'creditors were seen running away from their debtors, and debtors pursuing them in triumph, and paying them without mercy.'[92]

The case which, more than any other, tells the story of the ebbing of Marshall's dominance is *Ogden v. Sanders* (1827),[93] which carved the heart out of Marshall's *Sturges v. Crowninshield* opinion by upholding a bankruptcy law that applied only to debts incurred after the enactment of the statute. When such a statute is in effect at the time a contract is made, the Court held, the contract must be said to incorporate the statute. Therefore, since the bankruptcy provision of the statute is incorporated in the contract, the contract obligation is not impaired by its exercise. Marshall, dissenting, would have held that the obligations of even such subsequent contracts cannot be impaired by state bankruptcy laws.

Ogden v. Sanders substantially weakened the effectiveness of the contract clause as a barrier to economic reform by validating the application of reform legislation to later-executed contracts. It was not until the 1890's that this ground lost by the conservatives was recaptured by the birth of the concept that "unreasonable" reform legislation constitutes a deprivation of "liberty of contract" without due process of law. Pfeffer has described the significance of *Ogden v. Sanders* as follows:

> Sturges v. Crowninshield *was for all practical purposes destroyed by the Court in the case of* Ogden v. Sanders. *This was the first case in which Marshall suffered a defeat on a major constitutional issue, and his defeat was total. Even Bushrod Washington did not join him in his dissent. Marshall's dissent was bitter.*

---

92. Schlesinger, *The Age of Jackson*, at 30-31.
93. U.S. (12 Wheat.) 213 (1827).

The effect of the decision, he said, was to make 'prostrate...inanimate, inoperative and unmeaning' a vital provision of the Constitution 'on which the good and the wise reposed confidently.'[94]

The division on the Court in *Ogden v. Sanders* was indicative of the weakening of Marshall's hold on his Associates in the late 1820's. As will be recalled, a solid 5-2 conservative majority existed on the Bench until as late as 1823. The following year, Smith Thompson (1824-43) replaced Livingston. Thompson was somewhat more liberal than his predecessor. In 1826, Robert Trimble (1826-28), a moderate, replaced the conservative Todd. With these changes, the conservative majority was reduced to 4-3.

TABLE D

Alignment of Justices - 1826

Liberal	Moderate	Conservative
	Johnson	Marshall
	Thompson	Story
	Trimble	Washington
		Duval

The defection of only one conservative was enough to give the moderates a majority. In *Ogden*, the defector was Bushrod Washington, and the result was a 4-3 victory for Johnson, Thompson, Trimble, and Washington over Marshall, Story, and Duval.

A final comment is appropriate here regarding the struggle between Marshall and Jefferson that played such an important role in the first conservative era of Supreme Court history. Clearly Jefferson won the early rounds. From 1801 to approximately 1812, Jefferson and his Republican forces succeeded in intimidating the Marshall Court. The Chief Justice's strategy during the period was to wait patiently and to avoid open clash with the government's executive and legislative branches.

Marshall won the middle rounds. After Jefferson left office in 1809, the national mood shifted toward the nationalism and

---

94. Pfeffer, *This Honorable Court*, at 110.

economic conservatism that Marshall preferred. Marshall took advantage of the favorable social climate to write his personal views on many issues into law through a series of landmark cases culminating in the 1819 *Sturges-McCulloch-Dartmouth College* trilogy. Says Schlesinger:

> *This long and superb series of decisions written by Marshall, or under his influence, had pretty well established the Constitution as a document which forbade government interference with private property, even on the ground of the public welfare.*[95]

From retirement at Montecello, Jefferson sent out anguished protests, but Marshall clearly had the initiative.

Beginning with the crash of 1819, however, Marshall's dominance began to wane. *Ogden v. Sanders* suggests that Jeffersonian economic liberalism was once again taking control. No doubt Jefferson would have applauded Marshall's decline enthusiastically, but by 1827 he was dead. Marshall had outlasted his old enemy, only to see final victory slipping away during his waning years.

Marshall died in 1835. Near the end of his life, he grew very pessimistic about the future of his political and economic beliefs and the nation he loved so well. From the grave, Jefferson, his old antagonist, seemed to be having the last laugh. Conservatives were distraught over Marshall's demise. "Great, good and excellent man!" wrote Joseph Story of him, "I shall never see his like again.... Providence grants such men to the human family only on great occasions to accomplish its own great end."[96]

His pessimism notwithstanding, Marshall had built well. The battle between economic conservatism and liberalism was far from over in 1835. In that struggle, which has lasted to the present and which appears to be a perennial theme of Supreme Court history, the wily old Federalist had given to the conservatives major advantages and had delivered to the liberals major setbacks.

---

95. Schlesinger, *The Age of Jackson*, at 322.
96. 1 Warren, *The Supreme Court*, at 803, 813.

Part Three

The First Liberal Era (1836-1890)

Chapter Six

The Jackson/Taney Period (1836-1864)[97]

The age of American history dominated by Andrew Jackson marked the first time that populist sentiments became majority viewpoints on the Supreme Court. It has been said that in 1837, the year in which Jackson left office, "[T]he election of 1800...finally caught up with the Supreme Court."[98] As a result of Jackson's appointments, a modified form of the Jeffersonianism that had captured Congress and the Presidency but not the Court in the first decade of the nineteenth century became dominant on the Court as well.

The election of 1828 brought to power a group of men who were committed to making government the servant of the common people rather than the protector of the interests of the wealthy and privileged classes. These men, under Jackson's leadership, rode into office on the wave of discontent produced by the prolonged depression that began in 1819 and gave the 1820's the name "depression decade."

The Jacksonians believed the hard times of the 1820's were largely the result of selfish and irresponsible conduct by the banking community. The Jacksonian political program was centered upon breaking the nearly sovereign power of the existing banking system in order to create a financial system that would act on behalf of the entire people rather than solely on behalf of vested wealth. Probably the single greatest political event of the Jackson era was the veto of the United States Bank, the predominantly private institution that had exercised essentially unrestrained control over American high finance.

97. Material in this chapter is based largely on Schlesinger, *The Age of Jackson*, and 2 Warren, *The Supreme Court*, 1-357.
98. Pfeffer, *This Honorable Court*, at 126.

This veto marked the climax of a "battle between antagonistic philosophies of government: one declaring that property should control the state; the other denying that property had a superior claim to government privileges and benefits."[99]

In this struggle between the classes, the Jacksonians explicitly sided with the have-nots. Amos Kendell, Jackson's closest political advisor, summarized his faction's philosophy this way:

> In all civilized as well as barbarous countries, a few rich and intelligent men have built up Nobility Systems; by which, under some name, and by some contrivance, a few are enabled to live upon the labor of the many.... [These ruling classes] are founded on deception and maintained by power. The people are persuaded to permit their introduction, under the plea of public good and public necessity. As soon as they are firmly established, they turn upon the people, tax and control them by the influence of monopolies, the declamation of priest-craft and government-craft, and in the last resort by military force.[100]

The Jacksonians reversed the Federalist views on government and economics and held that the task of government was to restrain the rich in their assaults upon the poor. Marcus Morton, who then served on the Massachusetts Supreme Court, expressed the radical Jacksonian position in the following statement:

> My opinion is that the danger most to be feared and guarded against is encroachment by the powerful upon the weak - and by the rich upon the poor - and not the reverse. My constant apprehension is that the weaker members of the community will be divested of, or restricted in their rights. The greatest vigilance is needed to protect the common mass of the community - the industrious, quiet, producing classes of Society - against the overbearing influence of the rich and

99. Schlesinger, The Age of Jackson, at 92.
100. Quoted in id. at 97.

powerful.... If I am not always found on the side of the weak against the strong, whether in reference to Government, corporations or people, it will be because I err in finding which that side is.[101]

The Jacksonian political revolution, in contrast to Jefferson's, succeeded in capturing the Supreme Court. This was due, in large part, to the fact that Jackson made as many appointments to the Bench in eight years as Jefferson, Madison, and Monroe made in 24.[102] The Jackson Justices also received substantial support from the appointees of subsequent Jacksonian Presidents Martin Van Buren and James K. Polk.

The first liberal era of Supreme Court history was ushered in by the 1836 appointment of Chief Justice Roger B. Taney (1837-64). Taney's ascension to the Bench was important for at least three reasons. First, it gave Jackson's appointees, for the first time, a Court majority. Second, it marked the departure of the venerable Marshall. Third, it brought to the Court the most forceful and articulate champion of popular rights in its 45-year history.

Prior to 1837, Taney had been a central figure in Jackson's administration and one of its most consistent radical democrats. He was selected to serve as attorney general in 1831. As a member of Jackson's inner circle, he played a key role in the President's war against the dominance of the wealthy classes over American politics. He was a staunch opponent of the United States Bank. He strongly encouraged Jackson in the decision to veto the Bank's charter. He drafted the major portion of the veto message which Schlesinger contends, "burst like a thunderclap over the nation." The message stated in part:

---

101. Quoted in *id.* at 171.

102. The number was six. John McClean (1830-61) succeeded the moderate Trimble and served for 31 years. Henry Baldwin (1830-44) replaced the conservative Bushrod Washington and served for 15 years. James M. Wayne (1835-67) took over William Johnson's seat and served for more than 30 years. Philip B. Barbour (1836-41) served only six years, but made key contributions during that time including the important opinion in New York City v. Miln, 36 U.S. (11 Pet.) 102 (1837). John Catron (1837-65) was appointed to fill a newly created seat just before the end of Jackson's presidency and served for nearly 30 years. Most important, however, was the appointment of Chief Justice Roger B. Taney (1837-64), who replaced John Marshall and remained on the Court for 27 years.

It is to be regretted that the rich and the powerful too often bend the acts of government to their selfish purposes. Distinction in society will always exist under every just government. Equality of talents, of education, or of wealth cannot be produced by human institutions. In the full enjoyment of the gifts of Heaven and fruits of superior industry, economy, and virtue, every man is equally entitled to protection by law; but when the laws undertake to add to these natural and just advantages artificial distinctions...to make the rich richer and the potent more powerful, the humble members of society - the farmers, mechanics, and laborers - who have neither the time nor the means of securing like favors to themselves, have a right to complain of the injustice of their government. [103]

Subsequently, after two Secretaries of the Treasury had refused to withdraw federal deposits from the Bank, Taney accepted an appointment to that position and withdrew the deposits. Taney's economic liberalism was the subject of the following comment which appeared in a newspaper at the time of his seating on the Supreme Court: "Mr. Taney is as sincere and thorough a Democrat as any in the country.... [H]e is a sound anti-monopoly Democrat." [104]

The liberal Taney's replacement of the conservative Marshall was only one component of the liberalization of Court personnel that began with Jefferson's 1804 appointment of William Johnson, continued throughout Jackson's presidency, and extended at least until 1845 when Story resigned. [105] For ex-

---

103. Quoted in Schlesinger, *The Age of Jackson*, at 90.

104. Quoted in 2 Warren, *The Supreme Court*, at 12. Taney's ability as a constitutional lawyer was evaluated by Benjamin R. Curtis, also a Supreme Court Justice and a very able constitutional lawyer, as follows: "His power of subtle analysis exceeded that of any man I ever knew...in his case balanced and checked by excellent common sense and by great experience in practical business, both public and private." Quoted in 2 Warren, *The Supreme Court*, at 13.

105. Jackson's first three Justices did little to liberalize the Court. In 1830, the moderate Robert Trimble was succeeded by John McLean (1830-61), a conservative, and the conservative Bushrod Washington was succeeded by Henry Baldwin (1830-44), a moderate who later claimed to have stood alone against Marshall's conservatism when he first arrived on the Court. In 1835, the moderate William Johnson was succeeded by the rather conservative James M. Wayne (1835-67). Jackson's appointees became distinctly more liberal starting with Taney.

ample, the same year Taney was seated, the conservative Duval was replaced by Justice Phillip P. Barbour, another Jacksonian Democrat who espoused the states' rights philosophy that was the heart of the liberal Jackson/Taney jurisprudence.[106] The following table gives a rough picture of the balance of power on the Court on economic issues after the seating of Taney and Barbour:

TABLE E

Alignment of Justices - 1837

Liberal	Moderate	Conservative
Taney	Baldwin	Story
Barbour	Thompson	McLean
		Wayne

During Taney's first session as Chief Justice, the Court handed down a trilogy of important rulings.[107] The most noteworthy of the three, the *Charles River Bridge* case, has been aptly described as the "symbol of the dawn of a new era" in American constitutional law.[108] It stands out in United States Supreme Court history as a true landmark decision that summarizes and embodies with unusual clarity a major turning point in the development of the law. The opinion, which was Taney's first in the field of constitutional law, revealed a new and radical spirit substantially different from the jurisprudence that had dominated the preceding quarter century.

The facts of the *Charles River Bridge* case were these. For 50 years, bridge transportation across the Charles River from Boston to Charlestown, Massachusetts had been in the hands of an extremely profitable monopoly. A corporate charter of 1785 had granted to the Charles River Bridge Company authority to build and operate a toll bridge across the river.

---

106. John Quincy Adams characterized Barbour as a "shallow-pated wildcat...fit for nothing but to tear the union to tatters." Quoted in Schwartz, *From Confederation To Nation* (Baltimore, Md.: John Hopkins University Press, 1973), at 13.

107. Charles River Bridge v. Warren Bridge, 36 U.S. (11 Pet.) 419 (1837); Briscoe v. Bank of Kentucky, 36 U.S. (11 Pet.) 257 (1837); Mayor of New York City v. Miln, 36 U.S. (11 Pet.) 102 (1837). The importance of the three cases is reflected in the fact that they occupy four hundred pages in the United States Reports.

108. Pfeffer, *This Honorable Court*, at 123.

This company was controlled by a group of wealthy private owners. In 1828, the Democratically controlled Massachusetts legislature chartered a second corporation, the Warren River Bridge Company, to build a parallel bridge that was to become free as soon as sufficient tolls had been collected to pay construction and operating costs. Although the original charter of the Charles River Bridge Company did not explicitly grant a right to permanent monopoly, the company brought suit to enjoin the new bridge.

The case presented in unusually clear form the question whether the law was to serve the interests of the rich or the poor: would the Supreme Court enjoin the people from providing themselves with free transportation in order to preserve the profits of a monopoly dominated by the few and the wealthy? The case for Charles River Bridge Company was argued by Daniel Webster, who had worked with astounding success to ensure the primacy of property rights within the American constitutional system. Webster argued that the new charter impaired the charter rights of his corporate client by destroying the old charter's profitability and thus violated the Constitution's contract clause.

The Court held that the people of Massachusetts could proceed with their toll-free bridge. Taney's opinion rejected the contention that the legislature, in granting the corporate charter, had implicitly promised that neither it nor its successors would take any action which might reduce the corporation's profits. Speaking for the majority, Taney propounded his new image of government. The primary purpose of government, he said, is to promote the happiness and welfare of the people at large, not to protect the accumulated property of the wealthy few. When the two interests clash, it is not to be presumed that the good of the community must yield to the claims of the wealthy. As Taney stated:

> The object and end of all government is to promote the happiness and prosperity of the community by which it is established; and it can never be assumed that the government intended to diminish its power of accomplishing the end for which it was created.... A State ought never to be presumed to surrender this power because...the whole community have an in-

*terest in preserving it undiminished.... The continued
existence of a government would be of no great value,
if by implications and presumptions, it was disarmed
of the powers necessary to accomplish the ends of its
creation; and the functions it was designed to perform,
transferred to the hands of privileged corporations.*[109]

Pfeffer has described the importance of this decision as
follows:

> *This is a great opinion, on a par with Marshall's
> greatest, although proceeding from a diametrically op-
> posite political and economic predilection.... The
> prime purpose of government is no longer to protect
> private property and promote profit-making (as it was
> in the philosophy of Hamilton, Marshall and prac-
> tically all the fifty-five men who wrote the Constitu-
> tion); it is now to promote the welfare of the com-
> munity. The decision in favor of the free public bridge
> against the private profit-making bridge is one of the
> constitutional foundations of the social welfare
> legislation of the twentieth century.*[110]

The significance of the case was also not lost on Justice
Story, who felt that the decision amounted almost to a repeal
of the Constitution, since the fundamental purpose of the Constitution was, in his view, precisely to protect the rights of
the wealthy from this sort of attack. His private opinion was
that "a case of grosser injustice, or more oppressive legislation,
never existed."[111] No doubt in Marshall's prime the case would
have gone the other way. Indeed, the case had been argued
before Marshall's death, and all three pre-Jacksonian Justices
(Marshall, Story, and Thompson) were prepared to hold the
new charter unconstitutional.

Briscoe v. Bank of Kentucky,[112] the second member of the
1837 trilogy, also vividly demonstrated the economic
liberalism of the early Taney Court. A Kentucky statute had

---

109. Charles River Bridge v. Warren Bridge, 36 U.S. (11 Pet.) 419, 430-31 (1837).
110. *This Honorable Court,* at 125.
111. Quoted in Schlesinger, *The Age of Jackson,* at 326.
112. 36 U.S. (11 Pet.) 257 (1937).

authorized the issuance of promissory notes by a state-owned bank. The issue was whether the notes were "bills of credit" prohibited by the United States Constitution.[113] The Court held the notes were not bills of credit. The decision provided breathing room for the states in their efforts to combat the severe depression that had begun in 1837. Story dissented. He concluded that the Kentucky notes, like the loan certificates in *Craig v. Missouri*,[114] were unconstitutional.

Mayor of New York City v. Miln,[115] the last of the 1837 trilogy, also indicated the Court's new economic liberalism. A New York statute had required ship masters to submit to customs officials lists of all passengers in order to assist New York with problems concerning foreign papers. The Marshall Court's normal position was that local regulation of such matters should be restricted to as to minimize interference with interstate commerce. The Taney Court, on the contrary, upheld the local regulation. Speaking through Justice Barbour, the Court contended that a state has "not only the right, but the bounded duty...to advance the safety, happiness and prosperity of its people, and to provide for the general welfare by any and every act of legislation which it may deem conducive to these ends."[116]

This 1837 trilogy merits careful attention. Like its 1819 predecessor (*Sturges—McCulloch—Dartmouth College*), it symbolizes a particular era of the Court. Each of the three matters spoken to by the Taney Court presented to the Bench a "great long-pending constitutional case" that had troubled the Court for years.[117] Each raised the basic issue of the power of government vis-a-vis vested financial and corporate interests. In each, the Taney Court adhered to the liberal line. "In all three of these cases, Judge Story dissented, and stated that Marshall before his death concurred with his (Story's) views."[118]

In the years following *Charles River Bridge, Briscoe*, and *Miln*, the liberalization of the Court's Justices continued. In 1838, two economic liberals, John Catron (1838-65) and John McKinley (1838-52), were sworn in to fill new, congressionally

---

113. United States Constitution, art. I, sec. 10.
114. 29 U.S. (4 Pet.) 410 (1830), discussed in n. 91 *supra*.
115. 36 (11 Pet.) 102 (1837).
116. *Id.* at 98.
117. 2 Warren, *The Supreme Court*, at 27.
118. *Id.*

created seats. Catron was an acknowledged opponent of "accumulated wealth and privilege."[119] McKinley's anti-corporation populism was demonstrated by his noted circuit court decision holding that corporations could only do business in the state in which they were chartered.[120]

In 1841, the liberal Barbour was replaced by Peter V. Daniel (1841-60), who proved to be the most radical member of the liberal wing. Daniel was "the Court's extreme agrarian, the sworn enemy of...corporations, and banks; the extreme defender of states rights...."[121] He believed that banks were "the most vicious example of great corporate monopolies, cancerous growths which would destroy the country if not cut out,"[122] and he advocated complete abolition of all banks. His term on the Court was characterized by a consistent "opposition to any appeasement of corporations."[123] The following table shows the Court's liberal dominance after the seating of Daniel.

TABLE F

Alignment of Justices - 1841

Liberal	Moderate	Conservative
Daniel	Baldwin	Story
Taney	Thompson	McLean
McKinley		Wayne
Catron		

By 1843, Joseph Story was the only Justice remaining on the Court from the era of Marshall and the Federalists. Story, it will be recalled, was an economic conservative who believed that the main purpose of government was the protection of property holders against the poor and evil members of society. He had watched the development of Jacksonian doctrines on the Bench with a growing feeling that the Constitution was dead

---

119. 1 Friedman & Israel, *The Justices of the United States*, at 748-49.
120. On appeal to the Supreme Court, the case was Bank of Augusta v. Earle, 38 U.S. (13 Pet.) 519 (1839).
121. 1 Friedman & Israel, *The Justices of the United States*, at 800.
122. *Id.* at 797.
123. Schlesinger, *The Age of Jackson*, at 329.

and the nation headed for doom. At the time of Taney's appointment, Daniel Webster wrote, "Judge Story thinks the Supreme Court is *gone*, and I think so too."[124] A few years later, Story himself put it this way: "I am the last of the old race of Judges. I stand as their solitary representative, with a pained heart and a subdued confidence."[125]

Hindsight tells us that Story's forebodings, like those of Webster, Chancellor Kent, the conservative New York judge and legal commentator, and other arch-Federalists, were unduly gloomy. Nevertheless, they show that the Court's democratic jurisprudence was fully recognized and deplored by the wealthy classes and their partisans. When Story was replaced by Levi Woodbury (1845-51), the Jacksonian revolution in Court personnel was essentially complete.[126]

With Taney and his fellow liberals solidly entrenched on the Supreme Court, the fundamental legal concept that provided the keynote of the emerging democratic jurisprudence was that of "police power." According to this doctrine, governments are inherently invested with the general power to take action to promote the health, safety, and well-being of their citizens. Under Marshall, the police power was consistently inhibited in order to protect and preserve the rights of property. Under Taney, the Court became willing to grant government's legislative and executive branches much more latitude to exercise police power, and the Court rejected with greater frequency claims that state action illegally infringed the vested rights of the wealthy.

The significance of the police power concept has been well stated in the following quotation from Pfeffer:

> [T]he police power concept was not invented by Taney or his Court; it was known in Marshall's day. But then it was understood narrowly, as its name indicates, to refer to the power of states to preserve order and safety within their borders. Under Taney the idea was broadened considerably to encompass the general well-being of the people; it became a power to provide

---

124. Quoted in McCloskey, *The American Supreme Court*, at 82.
125. Quoted in Schlesinger, *The Age of Jackson*, at 327.
126. Levi Woodbury, prior to his appointment, was a member of Jackson's cabinet and a supporter of both the Bank veto and the withdrawal of federal deposits.

for the welfare of the community. But not only was the scope of the concept widened; equally important, it was accorded a high constitutional status. As the opinions in the Charles River *and* Miln *cases indicate, even if exercise of the police and power transgresses on some other constitutionally protected right, such as the right to the fulfillment of the obligation of contract or to engage in interstate commerce, it is not for that reason unconstitutional. Implicit in this is the assumption that not merely are the interests of the community superior to the rights of the individual, but also that the protection of private property and the promotion of profit making are not necessarily the only or even highest and overriding ends of government - an assumption completely alien to the philosophy of Hamilton, Jay, and Marshall.*[127]

There were limits, however, to the scope of the Supreme Court's Jacksonian revolution. Conservative fears of the Bench's new populist spirit were in large measure misplaced. When the dust stirred up by the 1837 trilogy settled, and the world did not end, it became apparent that the Taney Court had not thrown the Constitution, Marshall's legacy, or property rights into the fire. On the contrary, among the Taney Court's major achievements was that its Jacksonian Justices were able to pursue their populist goals while maintaining a substantial degree of continuity with the doctrines of the Marshall Court. As court historian Robert G. McCloskey has pointed out:

> *The legend of Taney and his brethren as radical democrats, hostile to property rights, nationalism, and Marshall's memory was stronger than the facts that would have emerged from a reading of the decisions themselves. But as the decisions finally were read and compared with those of Marshall's time, as the whole doctrinal course of the Taney Court was traced, it became apparent that the legend was badly misleading. The old jurisprudence had not been*

---

127. *This Honorable Court*, at 127.

broken down after all, or even very greatly altered: the claims of property were still well protected, the nation was not constitutionally fragmented, judicial power was not surrendered.[128]

A decision illustrating the continuity between the Marshall and Taney Courts, and the latter's residual economic conservatism, is *Bronson v. Kinsie* (1843).[129] Supreme Court historian Charles Warren has supplied a detailed description of the case's background:

> *[A] recent statute of Illinois provided that a mortgagor's equity should not be lost for twelve months after foreclosure sale and that no sale should occur unless two thirds of the appraised value should be bid for the property. This was one of the many statutes which had been the outcome of the frightful state of business and finance then prevalent. The country had just passed through the panic of 1837; it was in the midst of the era of State bank failures and of State debt repudiations; scarcity of hard money had destroyed the inflated value of property; men who had debts to pay were forced to dispose of their property at ruinous prices to the few who had money to buy. As a consequence of these conditions, State after State had enacted statutes for the relief of debtors, stay-laws postponing collection of debts, laws granting exemption from execution and foreclosures of mortgages.*[130]

Here was a classic situation in which economic liberalism called for assistance to debtors in their time of dire need. Yet, in *Bronson*, the Taney Court held that the Illinois relief-law was a statute impairing the obligation of contracts and therefore void under the contract clause.[131]

---

128. McCloskey, *The American Supreme Court*, at 82-83.

129. 42 U.S. (1 How.) 311 (1843).

130. 2 Warren, *The Supreme Court*, at 102.

131. For other examples of economic conservatism in the heyday of the Taney Court, *see* Planters Bank v. Sharp, 47 U.S. (6 How.) 301 (1848), which held a Mississippi banking statute to be an unconstitutional impairment of contract rights, and Suydam v. Broadnax, 39 U.S. (14 Pet.) 67 (1840), which restricted application of state insolvency laws.

There are many reasons why the "liberal" Taney Court surprised its followers from time to time with conservative decisions. First, the Court, as an institution, tends to absorb its new members and remake them in its own image, particularly when the doctrines in question are the levers of the Court's own power. Furthermore, Marshall's prestige paradoxically increased rather than decreased with his death, since he died a mere mortal and was canonized as a saint and a sage. Most important, the ongoing surge of capitalism was too strong to be restrained by any branch of government, and capitalism demanded protection and security for property. The Taney Court, therefore, represents neither the nadir nor the zenith in the Supreme Court's cooperation with the propertied classes.

In addition, toward the middle of the 1800's, the Court's position on the rich/poor issue became complicated by the slavery issue that grew into a national obsession overshadowing all other topics. In this context, controversies affecting the rich and the poor, which had held center stage in the political arena, became a secondary matter, and boundaries of economic conservatism and liberalism blurred.

One major cause of this blurring is that the traditional party of the "common people," the Democratic Party, which had been formed by Jackson after the House of Representatives stole the 1824 election from him, drifted into a pro-slavery southern strategy that weakened its position as moral leader in the arena of economic reform. At the same time, the "progressive" impulse passed increasingly to the Federalists' successors, the Whig Party, and later the Republican Party, groups which despite their anti-slavery views still tended to favor business interests.

The infamous 1857 *Dred Scott* case[132] amply illustrates this growing ambiguity. Here the Court's entire "liberal" wing (Taney, Daniel, Catron, and Campbell), all of whom were Southernors, concurred in the reactionary decision denying that black people, free and slave, were citizens who could bring lawsuits and holding that the federal government had no power to prohibit the extension of slavery into new geographical areas. The Court's two most economically conservative members, McClean and Curtis, dissented. Increasingly, as the

---

132. Scott v. Sandford, 60 U.S. (19 How.) 393 (1857).

years passed, the pro-slavery faction became wedded to a radical states' rights philosophy that was held to be the key to the continuation of slavery. This commitment was so strong as to subordinate the Justices' economic liberalism and to lead to states' rights decisions even where the result was to favor the rich over the poor.

In spite of the ambiguities and distortions created by the slavery issue, however, it seems safe to conclude that, overall, the Court at mid-century continued the tradition of economic liberalism inherited from the Jackson era. Chief Justice Taney, leader of the Jacksonian wing, remained in office until 1864. The radical Daniel served until 1860, and his replacement, Samuel F. Miller (1862-90), was also an economic liberal. As late as 1860, the balance of power on economic issues still tended to reside in the Court's liberal wing, as the following table shows:

TABLE G

Alignment of Justices - 1860

Liberal	Moderate	Conservative
Taney	Grier	McLean
Daniel	Nelson	Wayne
Catron	Clifford	
Campbell		

For these reasons, it is appropriate to consider the entire period from Taney's seating in 1837 to his death in 1864 as an "era" of Court history during which economically liberal policies inherited from Jackson usually dominated the Court.[133]

Before turning away from this era, a final look should perhaps be taken at the two great Chief Justices, Marshall and Taney, since they embodied with particular clarity the two

---

133. To make the story complete, here is a brief identification of other new Justices who arrived on the Court around mid-century. In 1845, the moderate Smith Thompson was succeeded by Samuel Nelson (1845-72), another moderate, who had been Chief Judge of New York's highest state court. In 1846, the moderate Baldwin was succeeded by Robert C. Grier (1846-70), a moderate. In 1851, the moderate Woodbury was succeeded by Benjamin R. Curtis (1851-57), a conservative Boston lawyer. In 1858, Curtis was succeeded by Nathan Clifford (1848-81), a moderate conservative.

typical judicial attitudes toward the perennial economic and political struggle between the rich and the poor. For the conservative Marshall, government's fundamental role was to protect property rights against attacks by the poor. And he believed the judiciary's fundamental role in a constitutional democracy was to ensure that the masses could not, through their greater numbers at the polls, invade the vested rights of the wealthy few. For the liberal Taney, government's role was to promote the welfare of the community, the people, the masses. Where the special rights of the wealthy conflicted with the good of society as a whole, those rights must be viewed with suspicion and must be construed restrictively. Pfeffer provides an able summary of this dichotomy:

> The best of all possible worlds come about, in Marshall's philosophy, by rapid and boundless economic expansion. The surest way to achieve this is by allowing individual initiative free rein, and this can be done only by protecting property and property rights through forcefully restraining the predatory envy of the lower classes. To secure these ends governments are instituted among men deriving their just powers from the good, the wise and the rich. Taney, though also committed to the judicial protection of property rights, believed that 'the object and end of all government is to promote the happiness and prosperity of the community.' His ideas of the community and the obligations that government owes to it were completely beyond Marshall's realm of contemplation. Taney made of the concept of police power, barely known and severely limited by Marshall, an invaluable instrument for the effectuation of government's obligation to the community and a vehicle for social welfare legislation. To Marshall the Constitution and particularly the commerce and impairment of contracts provisions, sanctified and immortalized Adam Smith's Wealth of Nations; Taney's development of police power, a term not even found in the Constitution, provided the principal constitutional basis for America's present modified welfare state.

In short, Marshall was in complete harmony with the temper of the century of American history from the time of his death in 1835 until the coming of Roosevelt's New Deal, Taney with that of the twentieth century from the time of the coming of Franklin Roosevelt.[134]

---

134. Pfeffer, *This Honorable Court*, at 162.

Chapter Seven

The Court During the Post-Civil War Industrial Revolution (1865-1890)[135]

The post-Civil War era in the United States was a period of tremendous industrial expansion. Industrial capitalism, of course, was not entirely new to the nation. It had been systematically encouraged and protected by Hamilton and the Federalists. It had been given a strong boost by the War of 1812. And it had been sufficiently developed by the 1830's to give rise to intense struggles regarding factory working conditions and rights of employees to bargain collectively. Nevertheless, the nation that emerged from the Civil War was still an overwhelmingly rural, agricultural nation. During the post-Civil War era, the United States experienced its real industrial revolution, undergoing a period of extravagant economic growth that has earned the name "The Gilded Age."[136]

The Civil War itself gave a tremendous lift to American industry, igniting a boom that lasted until 1873. Leading the surge were the railroads, which had been started prior to the war and were in full expansion in the years after. Business enterprises of unprecedented size were undertaken and huge

135. Selection of 1865 as the start of a new phase in the Court's first liberal era is somewhat arbitrary. The primary justification is that the Civil War ended in that year. In addition, Taney died in the prior year, and the seating of his successor, Chief Justice Salmon P. Chase, marked the end of the revolution in Court personnel resulting from President Abraham Lincoln's five appointments. These changes will be described more fully below. The principal sources for material presented in this chapter are C. Peter Magrath, *Morrison R. Waite* (New York: The Macmillan Company, 1963); Arnold M. Paul, *Conservative Crisis and the Rule of Law* (New York: Harper Torchbooks, 1960), hereafter referred to as *Conservative Crisis*; Carl Brent Swisher, *Stephen J. Field* (Chicago: The University of Chicago Press, 1930); 2 Warren *The Supreme Court*, at 358-689.

136. 2 Richard Hofstadter, William Miller & Daniel Aaron, *The American Republic* (Englewood Cliffs, N.J.: Prentice-Hall, Inc., 1959), at 94-123.

fortunes amassed by such men as Commodore Vanderbilt of the New York Central and the "big four" of the Southern Pacific, Crocker, Hopkins, Huntington, and Stanford. Special favors granted by the systematically corrupt Grant administration (1869-77), such as the notorious agreement that allowed two imaginative profiteers, Jim Fisk and Jay Gould, to corner the gold market in 1869, added to the boom and increased the enormous profits of the entrepreneurs.

The surge of industrial development set in motion by the Civil War continued in spite of periodic panics and depressions. The post-War boom collapsed in the panic of 1873, which was followed by a depression lasting until nearly 1880. The result of the depression, however, was to increase the power of the strong companies by driving the weaker companies into bankruptcy. During the 1870's, for example, John D. Rockefeller put together his Standard Oil monopoly by destroying or taking over his competitors. Similarly, the recession of 1883 and the depression of 1893, while temporarily delaying industrial expansion, did not deflect it from its long term upward course.

The industrial revolution had certain specific social and economic results which are pertinent to the present study. First, the rich (or at least some of them) became richer. Fortunes far exceeding any previously seen in the United States were rapidly accumulated. Industrial growth was accompanied by increased concentration of wealth and power. In many fields, competition was almost completely eliminated, leaving control over vital goods and services in the hands of small groups of private individuals. Second, the plight of the poor (particularly the urban poor) was exacerbated. Impoverished city dwellers, their ranks swollen by large numbers of immigrants from abroad and migrants from rural areas, lived a Dickensian existence working in subhuman conditions for near starvation wages.[137]

The widening gap between the rich and the poor gave rise during the late 1800's to increasing class tensions. In order to defend their interests and redress the balance of power, the poor turned increasingly to federal and state legislatures, seeking the enactment of laws to regulate corporations and protect the little person. Reform oriented political movements appeal-

---

137. *Id.* at 260-87. Protective laws such as unemployment insurance, disability compensation, and welfare, of course, did not exist.

ing to the masses of the poor grew in strength as the years passed. These movements periodically caused conservative backlashes and gave rise to political counter-movements whose leaders opposed reforms and even denied that many reforms could be legally undertaken.

The fundamental question posed to the Supreme Court by the reform movement was whether legislative regulation of business activities constituted an unconstitutional infringement of the liberty and property of persons conducting those activities. As Professor Robert McCloskey put it, "[S]ince the gravest problem facing America was government regulation of business, that problem gradually became the major interest of America's constitutional court."[138] C. Peter Magrath, biographer of Chief Justice Morrison R. Waite (1874-88), has summarized the emergence of the economic regulation issue in the post-war era as follows:

> There was, for one thing, the whole question of economic regulation. By 1874, the outline of modern American society had clearly emerged; urban and industrial, it revealed great disparities of wealth and poverty, while small groups of men, accountable to no one, controlled the banks, railroads, and industries which were the economic sinews of the new nation. As those at the bottom of the economic scale felt the burdens of irresponsible economic power, there came demands for public regulation. First to protest were the western farmers who believed themselves oppressed by the giant railroad corporations. Those to be regulated naturally fought back, attacking the regulatory legislation on many fronts, but especially in the courts. From this conflict came some of the Court's most significant and difficult decisions.[139]

The post-war Court adopted a generally liberal approach to the resolution of this fundamental economic issue, allowing federal and state government substantial latitude to carry out economic reforms. President Abraham Lincoln's appointees were largely responsible for this posture. As the Jacksonians began to leave the Court, the task of replacing them fell to Lin-

138. McCloskey, *The American Supreme Court*, at 104.
139. Magrath, *Morrison R. Waite*, at 182-83.

coln, who made five appointments to the Bench during his four years in office.

Lincoln's first three appointments were economic liberals. In 1861, the conservative McLean left the Court. He was replaced by the moderate liberal Noah H. Swayne (1862-81), a Quaker and prominent Ohio attorney. Then Samuel F. Miller (1862-90) was chosen to succeed the radical Daniel. Miller, one of the giants of Supreme Court history, had been a country doctor before rising to fame as an Iowa attorney and leader of Midwest Republicanism. As a Justice, his opinions "reflected a hostility to corporate and financial wealth."[140] In 1862, Lincoln also selected his old Illinois friend, Eighth Circuit judge David Davis (1862-77), to succeed Campbell, who had resigned when his state seceded. Davis was Lincoln's most liberal appointee and the Court's most liberal Justice. His career was characterized by "opposition to corporate and financial interests."[141]

Lincoln's remaining two appointments were more conservative. A year after Miller and Davis took office, Stephen J. Field (1863-97) was selected to fill a newly created tenth seat on the Bench. Field, another giant of Supreme Court history, had moved to California in the 1849 gold rush, drafted California's basic statutory codes, and served on the California Supreme Court. A liberal in his early life, Field converted to ultra-conservatism and became one of the most conservative Justices in the history of the Court.[142] Next, after nearly 30 years of service, the liberal Taney died. Lincoln appointed as the new Chief Justice, Salmon P. Chase, whom Lincoln described as "about one and a half times bigger than any other man I ever knew."[143] Inexpert in the law and restive in his judicial robes, Chase turned out to be a mediocre Chief Justice and an economic moderate.

The Lincoln Court's liberal wing was further strengthened in

---

140. *Id.* at 99. Miller's liberalism is illustrated by the so-called Municipal Bond cases, in which the Court, for a change, rejected economic regulation over Miller's dissent. *Id.* at 210-11.

141. *Id.* at 99.

142. When the relatively liberal Catron left the Court in 1865, he was not replaced, so the Court was reduced again to nine Justices. The Catron/Field "succession" was clearly a conservative change.

143. 2 Warren, *The Supreme Court*, at 400. The reference is to Chase's character, not physical size.

1870, when President Ulysses S. Grant appointed Joseph P. Bradley (1870-92) to succeed the conservative Wayne. Bradley, another superstar of Supreme Court history,[144] was an eminent East Coast corporate lawyer who "showed marked independence toward the corporate interests he formerly defended, frequently upholding economic regulation."[145] He aligned himself in most cases with Miller and the liberals rather than with Field and the conservatives. In 1870, Grant also chose William Strong (1870-1880) to replace the moderate Grier. Strong, another railroad attorney, was a conservative who sided with Field on most economic issues.

To summarize, the general alignment on the Court after the seating of the Lincoln and Grant appointees was as follows:

TABLE H

Alignment of Justices - 1870

Liberal	Moderate	Conservative
Davis	Chase	Field
Miller	Nelson	Strong
Swayne	Clifford	
Bradley		

Although the liberal wing lacked an absolute majority, it was clearly the strongest bloc.

The post-war Court's economic liberalism, *i.e.*, its willingness to allow substantial legislative regulation of business, was revealed in the *Slaughterhouse Cases* of 1873,[146] the Court's first decision interpreting the critically important due process clause of the Constitution's fourteenth amendment, which had been ratified in 1868. At issue was a Louisiana statute granting a monopoly in the New Orleans slaughterhouse business to one corporation. Former Justice Campbell, who had resigned from the Court when Alabama seceded and had become an eminent member of the private

---

144. "With his powerful intellect and moral assertiveness, he surpassed all but a handful of judges who have sat upon the Court." 2 Friedman & Israel, *The Justices of The United States*, at 1200. "Bradley was later to prove one of the strongest members of the bench, on a par with Miller and Field." Pfeffer, *This Honorable Court*, at 185.

145. Magrath, *Morrison R. Waite*, at 100.

146. 83 U.S. (16 Wall.) 36 (1873).

bar, argued for petitioners that the due process clause should be construed to prohibit unreasonable regulation of business. The arch-conservative Field agreed.

But the Court, speaking through its liberal leader, Justice Samuel F. Miller, rejected the argument and adopted a narrow reading of the due process clause. As long as economic reform legislation is enacted in compliance with proper legislative procedures, the Court held, it complies with the due process clause. In other words, the due process clause is "procedural," not "substantive." And although the immediate effect of the *Slaughterhouse Cases* was to preserve a hated monopoly, the liberal thrust of the decision was clear: the Supreme Court would not sit as a censor over economic reform legislation. The due process clause would not be construed as the source of power to nullify laws that the Justices might consider unsound or unreasonable.

During the same year in which the *Slaughterhouse Cases* was decided, Chief Justice Chase died and Associate Justice Nelson resigned. To replace Chase, President Grant chose Morrison R. Waite (1874-88). The Chase-Waite succession further strengthened the Court's liberal wing. Although he was an ex-business attorney, Chief Justice Waite normally voted to uphold economic reform legislation. Waite's biographer has summarized his attitude as follows: "Dislike for the rapaciousness of the new capitalism, confidence in the people's capacity to govern, and a feeling that the function of judges was properly a limited one were, then, the judicial and social attitudes which shaped Morrison Waite's response in economic cases."[147] To fill Nelson's seat, Grant selected Ward Hunt (1873-82), another moderate. Hunt, a former New York lawyer and judge, was a minor figure in Supreme Court history. Perhaps his most notable achievement was serving five years while mentally incompetent, until a special law was passed allowing him to retire at full salary.

The following table shows the balance of power on the Bench during the crucial period in the mid 1870's when the Court developed its position on the emerging issue of business regulation. Clearly the liberals had the edge.

---

147. Magrath, *Morrison R. Waite*, at 209.

TABLE I

Alignment of Justices - 1874-1877

Liberal	Moderate	Conservative
Davis	Clifford	Field
Miller	Hunt	Strong
Swayne		
Bradley		
Waite		

The question of the constitutionality of economic legislation was presented in its sharpest focus by legislation arising from the first major post-Civil War reform movement, the Granger Movement. This ferment, which began in 1867, was a collective effort by midwestern farmers to check certain abuses of economic power by the railroads.[148] Fed by the social unrest caused by the depression that began in 1873, the Granger Movement succeeded in obtaining reform legislation in a number of states. One such "Granger statute" was an Illinois measure regulating the rates that could be charged by certain grain elevators whose owners had obtained a stranglehold on the flow of grain from the midwestern farms to the eastern markets. The owners of the elevators challenged the law as an illegal infringement of their liberty to conduct business as they saw fit and of their property interest in maximizing their business profits.

The case that settled the legality of regulating Chicago grain elevator rates, *Munn v. Illinois* (1877),[149] is generally recognized by legal historians as the landmark case regarding the legality of economic reform legislation in the post-Civil War era. The Supreme Court, with only two dissents, upheld Illinois' authority to enact the regulatory legislation in question. Following in the tradition of Taney and the Jacksonians, the Court based its decision on the states' police power and held that when private property is used in such a way as to create a public interest in its use, it may be regulated in order to protect that public interest.

---

148. The principal abuses were excessive and discriminatory rates. The remedies demanded by the Grangers were (1) maximum rate limits, (2) equal and nondiscriminatory rates, and (3) prohibition of monopolies.

149. 97 U.S. 113 (1877).

The key passage in Chief Justice Waite's opinion for the Court is as follows:

> [T]he government regulates the conduct of its citizens one towards another, and the manner in which each shall use his own property, when such regulation becomes necessary for the public good.... Property does become clothed with a public interest when used in a manner to make it of public consequence, and affect the community at large. When, therefore, one devotes his property to a use in which the public has an interest, he, in effect, grants to the public an interest in that use, and must submit to be controlled by the public for the common good, to the extent of the interest he has thus created.[150]

This point was made even more forcefully by Justice Bradley in an outline he prepared to help Chief Justice Waite with the opinion:

> Whenever a particular employment, or a business establishment becomes a matter of public consequence so as to affect the whole public and to become a 'common concern' it is subject to legislative regulation and control. Whatever affects the community at large ought to be subject to such regulation, otherwise the very object of legislative power - the consulting of the general good - would be subverted. Unrestricted monopolies as to those things which the people must have and use, are a canker in any society, and have ever been the occasion of civil convulsions and revolutions. A people disposed for freedom will not tolerate this kind of oppression at the hands of private corporations or powerful citizens.[151]

The Waite Court's economic liberalism was by no means limited to the issue of rate regulation. Biographer Magrath has correctly pointed out that such a philosophical and political outlook was a general characteristic of this Bench:

---

150. *Id.* at 126.
151. Quoted in Magrath, *Morrison R. Waite*, at 182-83.

*In economic matters the Waite Court displayed in-
difference to the claims for special constitutional protection submitted by the nation's economic leaders.
For one thing, its judges lacked any real commitment
to the immense concentration of financial and corporate property which appeared after the Civil War.
For another, all of the fourteen men who at one time or
another made up the Waite Court (1874-89) grew to
maturity in Jacksonian America, and most of them retained their democratic faith.* [152]

As a result of their Jacksonian belief in regulating business to
serve the public interest, the Waite Court Justices, as a rule,
upheld economic reform legislation:

*Besides upholding state power to regulate railroads
and alter the right of creditors, the Waite Court sustained a variety of local regulatory laws despite
claims that they violated the Fourteenth
Amendment's due process clause, conflicted with the
commerce clause, or infringed on Congress' power
over interstate commerce. Quarantine regulations,
wharfage fees for public docks, prohibitions on the
sale and manufacture of liquor, and condemnation of
businesses that were a public nuisance all won
judicial approval. Laws repealing earlier grants of
monopolistic privileges were upheld in decisions taking a broad view of the states' police power.* [153]

The United States' rising corporate elite looked upon these
decisions with extreme disfavor. The following remarks -
which, according to Magrath, may have been inspired by Field -
provide an indication of the intensity of reaction among the
representatives of the corporate interests:

*No other decision [Munn v. Illinois] has ever been
made in the course of our judicial history, - not even
excepting the notorious Dred Scott case, - which*

---

152. *Id.* at 205.
153. *Id.* at 215.

*threatens such disastrous consequences to the future
wealth and prosperity of the country.... [I]ts doctrine
involves the very essence of the destructive theories
maintained by the socialists and communists of
France and Germany.... It is relied upon as an authority to sustain and validate the communistic legislation
already enacted by several of the States.... [T]he step
from the property of corporations to that of private
citizens is a short and easy one; it will soon and certainly be taken, for it has already been taken by the
Supreme Court. The Dred Scott case indirectly struck
at the stability of our political fabric; the Elevator case
directly strikes at the stability of private property, - at
rights which lie in the very foundation of modern
society and civilization.*[154]

By 1880, dislike for the Court was already sufficient to foment
an abortive effort, backed by railroad magnate Gould, to pack
the Court with pro-business conservatives.[155]

Despite growing corporate opposition, the Court's relative
economic liberalism continued into the 1880's. In 1877, the
Court's most liberal member, David Davis, resigned to pursue
his political ambitions, but he was succeeded by another
liberal, John Marshall Harlan (1877-1911). Harlan, a major
figure in Supreme Court history, promptly took over Davis'
place on the Court's liberal edge.[156] Thus, throughout the
period of Waite's Chief Justiceship, the proponents of
economic regulation had four relatively reliable supporters on
the Court: Miller, Bradley, Waite, and Davis/Harlan. The
liberal bloc normally could pick up the needed additional vote
and more from such moderates as William Woods (1881-87),
Stanley Matthews (1881-89), Horace Gray (1881-1902), and
Samuel Blatchford (1882-1902). As Magrath puts it:

---

154. John Norton Pomeroy, The Supreme Court and State Repudiation, 17 American
Law Review 684, 712 (1883).

155. This phase of Court history has been chronicled in Magrath, *Morrison R. Waite*, ch.
12, "Court-Packing in the Age of Enterprise," at 228-49 (1963).

156. Harlan was clearly the Court's most liberal member in civil liberties cases during
most of his tenure. On economic issues, Harlan's performance was more checkered. He frequently voted against labor's interests, for example. However, he also lined up with the
liberal wing on many rich/poor issues.

Justice Stanley Matthews, while sympathetic to property rights, did not - as the business elite had clearly expected - join Justice Field in protest against the majority's 'revolutionary course'.... His [President Chester Arthur, 1881-85] two appointments to the Court, Samuel Blatchford and Horace Gray, neither of whom fit the railroad attorney model, also aligned themselves with Waite on the major economic issues before the Court.[157]

Meanwhile, the nation continued to polarize over the issue of government regulation of business. Under the banner of Social Darwinism and laissez faire, conservative interests sought a free hand for the financial and industrial entrepreneurs, while the poor pressed for increased government control. The recession of 1883, while not as severe as the depressions of 1873 and 1893, gave rise to a period of social unrest with renewed demands for reform. During this period the labor movement experienced a major surge. Social tension reached a climax in 1886 when the Haymarket Square bombing left several dead and a large number wounded. Cries of anarchy and communism were again heard.

But the Court did not yet swing to the right. In 1887, for example, *Mugler v. Kansas,*[158] upheld a Kansas prohibition law as a valid exercise of police power. In his opinion for the majority, Harlan stated, "Under our system that power is lodged with the legislative branch of government. It belongs to that department to exert what are known as the police powers of the State, and to determine, primarily, what measures are appropriate or needful for the protection of the public morals, the public health, or the public safety."[159] This liberal view of police power was again in evidence in *Powell v. Pennsylvania,*[160] which upheld a state statute banning the sale of margarine.

During the 1870's and 1880's, opposition on the Bench to economic regulation was carried predominantly by Justice

157. Magrath, *Morrison R. Waite,* at 247.
158. 123 U.S. 623 (1887).
159. *Id.* at 660-61.
160. 127 U.S. 678 (1888).

Field. In his view, most attempts to regulate the conduct of business were reprehensible and unconstitutional invasions of the sacred rights of liberty and property.[161] Field's strong solicitude for the rich is revealed in numerous passages from his opinions. The following quotation, taken from his 1895 opinion denying the constitutionality of the federal income tax, is but one of many typical examples of his outlook:

> *The present assault on capital is but the beginning. It will be but the stepping-stone to others, larger and more sweeping, till our political contests will become a war of the poor against the rich; a war constantly growing in intensity and bitterness. If the Court sanctions the power of discriminating taxation, and nullifies the uniformity mandate of the Constitution, it will mark the hour when the sure decadence of our government will commence.*[162]

Field, with some support from Justice Strong and, occasionally, others, carried on a bitter and relentless fight against the Court's majority, a fight which was to lead to success in the 1890's when, with new personnel, the Court reversed itself and adopted Field's views.

In the twilight years of the period of judicial history that began in the days of Andrew Jackson and Roger B. Taney, and which we have termed the Supreme Court's first liberal era, one case in particular stands out as suggestive both of the state of existing law on the rich-poor issue and of the changes impending in the Bench's temperament: *Budd v. New York* (1892).[163]

---

161. Field's biographer has summarized Field's views on these matters as follows: "Again and again he stressed the importance of great corporations in the achievement of things that were worth while. Because of their importance he insisted upon their being protected to the full extent of the law. Nothing stirred his ire more quickly than short-sighted efforts to restrict corporate activities. Such efforts were, in his estimation, of a piece with the dictates of the vicious doctrines of socialism and communism, and it was the duty of the courts to bring about their frustration. Yet his interest seems not to have been in corporations as such, but rather in the achievements of men of vision and energy who used corporations as tools. His opposition, with but occasional exceptions, was to government interference with freedom of action in the business world. When business and industrial leaders garnered rich rewards for their labors, Field was ready to use the machinery of the law to protect them against the resentment and cupidity of the masses." Swisher, *Stephen J. Field*, at 396.

162. Pollock v. Farmers' Loan & Trust Co., 157 U.S. 429, 607 (1895).

163. 143 U.S. 517 (1892).

In *Budd*, the Waite Court's economic liberalism still prevailed but only over the increasingly strident opposition of the men who would soon provide the *dramatis personae* in one of the most significant Court turnabouts since 1790 and until the present.

The case involved a challenge to an 1888 New York rate regulation statute that set maximum rates to be charged by warehouses, grain elevators, and shippers along the crucial Erie Canal-Hudson River transportation system. The case was directly within the rule established by *Munn v. Illinois.* However, when heard earlier in the New York Court of Appeals, which upheld the law, a remarkable dissenting opinion was filed by Rufus W. Peckham, who only a few years later was to become a United States Supreme Court Justice. Here is what Peckham said:

> *To uphold legislation of this character is to provide the most frequent opportunity for arraying class against class; and, in addition to the ordinary competition that exists throughout all industries, a new competition will be introduced, that of competition for the possession of the government....*
>
> *In my opinion, the court should not strain after holding such species of legislation constitutional. It is so plain an effort to interfere with what seems to me the most sacred rights of property and individual liberty of contract that no special intendment in its favor should be indulged in....*
>
> *The legislation under consideration is not only vicious in its nature, communistic in its tendency, and in my belief, wholly inefficient to permanently attain the result aimed at, but, for the reasons already given, it is an illegal effort to interfere with the lawful privilege of the individual to seek and obtain such compensation as he can for the use of his own property.*[164]

Similar sentiments would not have been surprising coming from Field, but when *Budd* reached the Supreme Court, it was

---

164. 117 N.Y. 68, 69-71; 22 N.E. 670, 694-95 (1889).

a new Justice, David Brewer (1890-1910), who picked up Peckham's themes. Declaring in his dissent that the rule of *Munn v. Illinois* was "radically unsound,"[165] Justice Brewer stated:

> *The paternal theory of government is to me odious. The utmost liberty to the individual and the fullest possible protection to him and his property is both the limitation and the duty of government. If it may regulate the price of one service, which is not a public service, or the compensation for the use of one kind of property, which is not devoted to a public use, why may it not with equal reason regulate the price of all service, and the compensation to be paid for the use of all property? And if so, 'Looking Backward,' [Edward Bellamy's radical, utopian novel] is nearer than a dream.*[166]

Despite the thunderings of Peckham, Brewer, and Field, the New York rate regulation statute was upheld in a 6-3 decision. Thus, as late as 1892, Taney's concept of police power still prevailed over the emerging concept of liberty of contract. But the voices of dissent were growing louder and stronger.

---

165. Justice Field, of course, concurred in Brewer's dissent.
166. 143 U.S. 517, 551 (1892).

Part Four

The Second Conservative Era (1890-1937)

Chapter Eight

The First Age of Laissez Faire (1890-1905)[167]

The preceding chapter described the socio-economic patterns that emerged after the Civil War and typified America's industrial revolution. Industrial expansion and concentration gave rise to private businesses of unprecedented wealth and power. At the same time, urbanization, immigration, and industrialization produced a class of factory workers who lived in unprecedented poverty. To many observers, the traditional legal image of self-sufficient individuals dealing with each other in a context of independence and equality simply did not fit this new situation. Increasing demands were voiced for reform legislation designed to insure that private enterprise did not operate in a manner contrary to the interest of the people.

The traditional images, however, did not like old soldiers simply fade away. On the contrary, they took even stronger root among conservative groups that included the bulk of the rich and especially the entrepreneurs of the new industrial system. The politics of conservatism centered on the concept of laissez faire, i.e., the idea that government should keep its hands off business and let the economy go. This, in turn, was based on the twin pillars of Social Darwinism and Adam Smith's "invisible hand."

---

167. The beginning and ending dates of this period are somewhat arbitrary. Clearly there was a conservative period during the last decade of the 19th and first decade of the 20th centuries. The starting point, however, could be placed as early as 1888 or as late as 1893, and the end could be placed as late as 1910. The principal sources for the material presented in this chapter are Willard L. King, *Melville Weston Fuller* (Chicago: The University of Chicago Press, 1950); Paul, *Conservative Crisis*, and Swisher, *Stephen J. Field*.

According to Social Darwinism, "survival of the fittest" was the mechanism by which the human race advances, and any attempt to ameliorate the struggle for survival by helping the weak and the poor would only lead to long-term harm. Moreover, Adam Smith's *Wealth of Nations* assured the Social Darwinists that the forces of self-interest, if left unregulated, would lead to the greatest good for the greatest number as if guided by an invisible hand. To the conservatives, the new reform doctrines that emerged in the late 1800's were abhorrent concepts that threatened to subvert the most basic values of the American tradition.

During the 1890's, social forces pushed the reform and conservative viewpoints into increasing polarization.[168] From the beginning of the decade on, events moved toward a state of social tension and crisis. By the late 1880's, recovery from the recession that began in 1883 was complete. 1888 and 1889 were years of relative prosperity. By 1892, however, the pressure on the political system by advocates of reform had again become very intense:

> In that year [1892] the newly founded Populist party, catalyzing the rising agrarian unrest, prepared to challenge the major parties in the fall elections. The platform of the party...served as a rallying point for much of the protest and reformist movement. In addition to such standard agrarian demands as the free coinage of silver and credit inflation, the platform also demanded government ownership of railroads, telegraph and telephone, a graduated income tax, and the extension of the eight-hour day. The adoption of the platform was followed by a wild demonstration of six thousand people, described by one reporter as 'one of the most exciting scenes ever witnessed in a political convention.'
>
> Then...(just two days later) the widespread labor unrest of the early 1890's erupted violently at the Carnegie steel works in Homestead, Pennsylvania, when strikers of the Amalgamated Association of Iron

---

168. These developments have been carefully chronicled by Arnold M. Paul. The discussion that follows relies heavily on his anlaysis.

*and Steel Workers fought a pitched battle with three
hundred Pinkerton guards.*[169]

The result of these events of the early 1890's was "a general
hardening of conservative attitudes."[170]

Then followed the panic of 1893 and the beginning of a
severe depression "which in the course of the next few years
would exacerbate class antagonism in every sphere of social
life."[171] As the depression deepened in 1894, the tension between the reformers and the conservatives moved toward a
climax. Coxey's "armies" (groups recruited by Jacob S. Coxey
from the more than 2,000,000 unemployed in the nation)
marched on Washington, receiving enthusiastic welcomes
from the Populist governors of several midwestern states. To
the conservatives, Coxey's armies, like Shays' Rebellion of
1786, appeared as an eruption of the forces of anarchy.

But even Coxey's armies paled in comparison to the threat
unleashed by renewed labor militancy. During 1894, over
700,000 workers were out on strike. The most celebrated instance of this labor activity was the Pullman strike led by
Eugene V. Debs:

> *And on May 11, 1894 began the famous strike at
> Pullman, Illinois; with the entrance into the fray on
> June 26 of the 150,000 men of the American Railway
> Union, organized for aggressive action and determin-
> ed to make the strike a major test of labor solidarity,
> the conflict of the 1890's between capital and labor
> came to its climax.*[172]

As the social tension and demands for reform intensified, the
conservative backlash intensified as well. The growing conservatism of the mid-1890's can be illustrated by the following
quotation from Theodore Roosevelt (an individual often claimed as a hero by the progressive movement and therefore
presumably not representative of the far right) regarding

---

169. Paul, *Conservative Crisis*, at 75.
170. *Id.* at 76.
171. *Id.* at 82.
172. *Id.* at 130.

William Jennings Bryan and other leaders of the Democratic campaign in the election of 1896:

> *I speak with the greatest soberness when I say that the sentiment now animating a large proportion of our people can only be suppressed, as the Commune in Paris was suppressed, by taking ten or a dozen of their leaders out, standing them against a wall, and shooting them dead. I believe it will come to that. These leaders are plotting a social revolution and the subversion of the American Republic.*[173]

Gradually at first, but then with gathering momentum, the conservative backlash of the 1890's swept the Supreme Court far to the right. Here is how one important historian of the era, Arnold M. Paul, has described the shift:

> *In the 1890's the pressures on the Court came from large propertied interests who opposed social reform, labor unionism, and economic regulation they could not control. Moderate traditionalists on the bench, misconstruing the social tensions of protest and depression as the coming majoritarian radicalism, succumbed to these pressures. The Supreme Court (and the judiciary in general) moved to the right, buttressed the ideological rigidities of laissez faire, and carried through a conservative-oriented constitutional revolution.*[174]

Although the proponents of police power retained substantial strength on the Supreme Court until the 1890's, the tide began to turn inexorably toward judicial enthronement of laissez faire in the 1880's. As late as March 1888, the Court had four members (Waite, Miller, Bradley, and Harlan) who normally voted to uphold economic reform legislation, and only one member (Field) who can be characterized as an extreme conservative on economic issues. By 1896, the situation had

---

173. Quoted in Henry F. Pringle, *Theodore Roosevelt* (New York: Harcourt, Brace & World, Inc., 1931), at 114.

174. Paul, *Conservative Crisis*, at xiv - xv.

exactly reversed, and a solid four-vote conservative bloc (Field, Brewer, Peckham, and Fuller) confronted a liberal wing that had been reduced to one (Harlan).

The first major change occurred when Chief Justice Waite died in March 1888 and was replaced by Melville W. Fuller (1888-1910). Although not as doctrinaire as Field, Brewer, and Peckham, the new Chief Justice was a conservative on economic issues.[175] Shortly thereafter, in January 1890, David Brewer was sworn in to replace the moderate Matthews. Brewer was Field's nephew and, like his uncle, an extreme advocate of laissez faire conservatism.[176] The following excerpts from Brewer's 1891 Yale University commencement address demonstrate his commitment to the protection of property rights:

> *From the time in earliest records, when Eve took loving possession of even the forbidden apple, the idea of property and the sacredness of the right of its possession have never departed from the race. Whatever dreams may exist of an ideal human nature...actual human experience, from the dawn of history to the present hour, declares that the love of acquirement, mingled with the joy of possession, is the real stimulus to human activity. When, among the affirmatives of the Declaration of Independence, it is asserted that the pursuit of happiness is one of the unalienable rights, it is meant that the acquisition, possession and enjoyment of property are matters which human government cannot forbid and which it cannot destroy....*[177]
>
> *It [the police power] is the refuge of timid judges to escape the obligations of denouncing a wrong, in a case in which some supposed general and public good is the object of legislation.... I am here to say to you, in no spirit of obnoxious or unpleasant criticism upon*

---

175. *See, e.g.*, King, *Melville Weston Fuller*; 2 Friedman & Israel, *The Justices of the United States*, at 1515-23. "In sum, he was a conservative *laissez faire* Justice, less reactionary than some of his brethren, more compassionate than others, but a spokesman for what now seems a far-off and bygone age." *Id.* at 1481.

176. *See* p. 82 *supra.*

177. Quoted in Paul, *Conservative Crisis*, at 70-71.

*the decision of any tribunal or judge, that the
demands of absolute and eternal justice forbid that
any private property, legally acquired and legally held,
should be spoliated or destroyed in the interests of
public health, morals or welfare without compensation.*[178]

Professor Arnold Paul, a careful student of the 1890's, has
suggested that these two appointments (Fuller and Brewer)
resulted in a noticeable shift to the right in the Court's position on economic issues as early as 1890:

*The case [Chicago, Milwaukee & St. Paul Ry. Co. v.
Minnesota, 134 U.S. 418 (1890)] was also significant in
that it was the first indication of how recent changes
in personnel might have affected the Court's views.
Chief Justice Morrison R. Waite, a staunch defender of
the police power, had died in 1888, to be replaced by
Melville W. Fuller of Illinois. And in 1889, Justice
Stanley Matthews, a moderate conservative of states'
rights leaning, had been succeeded by David J. Brewer
of Kansas, already known for his refusal to follow the
Munn case as a United States Circuit Judge. Both
Fuller and Brewer, the latter the nephew of Justice
Field, were soon to find themselves within the ex-
treme conservative wing of the Court, reinforcing the
position that Field had long held alone.*[179]

The shift to the right accelerated during the nineteenth century's last decade when the Court lost two of its strongest
liberal Justices. In 1890, Miller died. His successor, Henry B.
Brown (1891-1906), although by no means an arch-
conservative, was neither as dominant nor as liberal a figure as
Miller.[180] In 1892, Joseph P. Bradley also died. His replacement,

---

178. *Id.* at 71.
179. *Id.* at 42.
180. *See, e.g.,* 2 Friedman & Israel, *The Justices of the United States,* at 1553-63, which
suggests that although Brown thought of himself as a conservative, he was one of the more
moderate members of the extremely conservative Court of the 1890's. "There is no doubt
that as a Supreme Court Justice Brown usually took the center position. He was neither a
liberal nor a reactionary...." *Id.* at 1557.

George Shiras, Jr. (1892-1903), was a moderate conservative who, to cite one pertinent example, provided the fifth vote that invalidated the income tax in 1895.[181]

After a few additional appointments that did not particularly affect the Bench's economic complexion,[182] the conservative revolution in Court personnel was completed in 1896, when Rufus W. Peckham (1896-1909) replaced Howell Jackson. Peckham, the New York judge who strongly dissented from the lower court decision in *Budd v. New York*,[183] was another arch-conservative and moved directly into the Court's far right wing with Field and Brewer.

With Peckham's confirmation, the Court reached, for the time being, the other extremity of its swing to the right. The following table shows the line-up of Justices after Peckham's seating:

TABLE J
Alignment of Justices - 1896

Liberal	Moderate	Conservative
Harlan	White	Field
	Shiras	Brewer
	Brown	Peckham
	Gray	Fuller

Even Harlan, who was quite liberal on civil rights cases, was arguably only a moderate on purely economic issues. For the conservatives, then, the mid-1890's were a shining moment with Field, Brewer, Peckham, and Fuller controlling the Court

181. Shiras has been labelled "middle-of-the-road." 2 Friedman & Israel, *The Justices of The United States*, at 1577. However, "(w)hen we observe Shiras' position on national regulatory power, we find him definitely on the right, close to the ultraconservative bloc in annulling or construing narrowly federal reform legislation." *Id.* at 1584.

182. The additional appointments were the following. Justice Woods had died in 1887. His replacement, the conservative Lucius Q.C. Lamar (1888-93), served only five years and was succeeded by Howell Jackson (1893-95). Samuel Blatchford died in 1893 and was succeeded by Edward D. White (1894-1921), a major figure in the Court's history, who became Chief Justice when Fuller died in 1910. "The judicial whimsy indicated by Justice White's erratic pattern in these basic substantive due process cases should not obscure the fact that White tended to vote conservatively, especially as he grew older." 2 Friedman & Israel, *The Justices in the United States*, at 1645.

183. See p. 81 *supra*.

and writing the doctrines of Social Darwinism and laissez faire into the fundamental law of the nation.

Returning to the late 1880's, the economic conservatism that was soon to be expressed by the Supreme Court can be seen emerging, particularly in state court decisions holding that efforts to regulate business activity were illegal deprivations of "liberty of contract"[184] and that strikes by organized labor were "criminal conspiracies" subject to injunction.[185]

On the Supreme Court, glimmers of the new conservatism were seen as early as 1890 when in the previously mentioned *Chicago, Milwaukee & St. Paul Ry. Co. v. Minnesota* case,[186] the Bench held unconstitutional a Minnesota rate regulation statute that purported to make rate decisions of the state regulatory commission final and to deny any right to judicial review. The opinion of the Court laid down the crucial doctrine that, *Munn v. Illinois* notwithstanding, the question of the reasonableness of rates was for the Court to determine.[187]

It was 1895, however, that marked the climax of the constitutional revolution that placed the philosophy of laissez faire in control of the judicial system.[188] In that year, the Court handed down another trilogy of famous cases comparable in importance and symbolic significance to the 1819 and 1837 trilogies discussed in earlier chapters.

---

184. The proponents of "liberty of contract" argued that laissez faire was a blessing to the poor in that it gave them the "opportunity" to be self-reliant and to pull themselves out of their plight without any help from anyone. For example: "It (a scrip act) is a species of sumptuary legislation which has been universally condemned, as an attempt to degrade the intelligence, virtue and manhood of the American laborer, and foist upon the people a paternal government of the most objectionable character, because it assumes that the employer is a knave and the laborer an imbecile." State v. Goodwill, 33 W.Va. 179 (1889).

185. That the class nature of the 1890's social conflict of was recognized on the Supreme Court is made clear in the following statement by Justice Henry B. Brown, previously quoted at p. 12 supra. "The history of civilized society is largely a story of strife between those who have and those who have not." Social conflict, the Justice continued, is largely a result of "the desire of the rich to obtain the labor of the poor at the lowest possible terms, the desire of the poor to obtain the uttermost farthing from the rich. The cause and the result of it all is the unequal distribution of property." Quoted in Paul, *Conservative Crisis*, at 85.

186. 134 U.S. 418 (1890).

187. Just a few years later, the Court first exercised its power to set aside railroad rates established by a state commission. Reagen v. Farmers' Loan & Trust Co., 154 U.S. 362 (1894).

188. "The year 1895 marked the crest for right-wing judicial conservatism." 3 Friedman & Israel, *The Justices of the United States*, at 1525. "The Fuller Court reached the peak of its commitment to the conservative cause in 1895...." *Id.* at 1485.

This trilogy began with *United States v. E.C. Knight Co,*[189] a case that nearly destroyed the ability of the federal government to combat monopoly within the private sector. In 1890, Congress had enacted one of the most potentially important pieces of economic reform legislation to that date, the Sherman Antitrust Act, which gave the Justice Department the power to seek injunctions against monopolies and restraints of trade. The Justice Department thereupon brought suit to force dissolution of the monopolistic sugar trust that controlled over 90 percent of the nation's sugar refining capacity. Speaking through Chief Justice Fuller, the Court held that the action could not be maintained. The Sherman Act, Fuller reasoned, was enacted pursuant to the commerce clause. However, the suit, he continued, was directed not at "commerce," i.e., transportation and sales, but at "manufacturing" and therefore was not within the scope of the commerce power. Manufacturing was a "local" activity reserved by the tenth amendment for exclusive state control. This decision eliminated the United States government's authority to control the conduct of manufacturing corporations.

The second and equally dramatic blow fell later that year when the Court, in *Pollock v. Farmers' Loan & Trust Co.,*[190] held that Congress was without power to impose a graduated income tax. Joseph H. Choate, lead counsel for the opponents of the tax, evoked the spirits of anarchy and communism and prophesied the end of civilization if the tax were allowed to stand:

> *The Act...is communistic in its purposes and tendencies, and is defended here upon principles as communistic, socialistic - what shall I call them - populistic as ever have been addressed to any political assembly in the world...*
>
> *I have thought that one of the fundamental objects of all civilized government was the preservation of private property. I have thought that it was the very keystone of the arch upon which all civilized government rests, and that this once abandoned, everything*

---

189. 156 U.S. 1 (1895).
190. 157 U.S. 429 (1895).

was in danger.... According to the doctrines that have been propounded here this morning, even that great fundamental principle has been scattered to the winds.[191]

The Court responded by overturning a century of authority and invalidating the tax. The effect of the decision was to prevent all graduated taxation of income until 1913, when the progressive era finally succeeded in passing the sixteenth amendment explicitly allowing such taxes.

The third key decision of 1895 was *In Re Debs*,[192] which upheld the labor injunctions issued in the Pullman strike of 1894. This ruling, which approved the use of courts as a means of preventing collective action by organized labor, completed the Court's rout, at least on a temporary basis, of populist programs for economic reform:

> *And on May 27, one week after the* Pollock *decision, the Supreme Court handed down its opinion in the* Debs *case, bestowing its official sanction on the new uses of the labor injunction.... The judicial developments of the spring of 1895 marked at last the acceptance of that judicial guardianship so determinedly advocated by right-wing conservatism.*[193]

Robert H. Jackson, a Supreme Court Justice serving from 1941 until 1954, has provided an analysis that highlights the drastic effect on the reform movement of the three 1895 decisions.[194] He points out that there are three basic ways in which government can undertake the task of redressing the balance of power that normally favors the rich against the poor: (1) by redistributing wealth from the rich to the poor through taxes, (2) by regulating activities of the rich, and (3) by encouraging the poor to unite in order to gain bargaining power through numbers. He states:

---

191. *Id.* at 532-34.
192. 158 U.S. 564 (1895).
193. Paul, *Conservative Crisis*, at 219.
194. Jackson, *The Struggle For Judicial Supremacy*, at 39-40.

*The central problem of democratic government
became one of working out a tolerable balance among
these forces (industry, finance, agriculture, and labor),
of moderating the always threatening power of those
whom society permits to own or control its economic
resources.... Our history demonstrates that our
legislatures saw the answer roughly in this way: first,
there must be a tax policy, based on ability to pay, sufficient to support social services for those upon whom
systematic inequalities bore most harshly - in short,
an income tax; secondly, there must be regulation of
the power of wealth where the premise of competition
failed; thirdly, those without wealth must be protected in their efforts to organize.*[195]

The 1895 trilogy struck directly at each of these fundamental methods of reform activity. The *Pollock* decision denied
government the power to   impose an income tax. The *E.C.
Knight* decision denied government the power to regulate the
activities of the great manufacturing corporations, including
the monopolistic trusts. The *Debs* decision denied the right of
workers to strike collectively in support of their demands.
Thus, the rulings of 1895 were tantamount to a systematic
judicial assault on the methods available to the poor in their
quest for greater justice.

These three decisions were received with scorn and fury by
the advocates of reform. The observations of Justice Brown in
his dissenting opinion in *Pollock* are illustrative of their concerns:

*[The Court's decision] involves nothing less than a
surrender of the taxing power to the moneyed class....
Even the spectre of socialism is conjured up to frighten
Congress from laying taxes upon the people in propor-
tion to their ability to pay them. It is certainly a
strange commentary...that Congress has no power to
lay a tax which is one of the main sources of revenue*

---

195. *Id.*

*of nearly every civilized State.... I hope it may not
prove the first step toward the submergence of the liberties of the people in a sordid despotism of wealth.*[196]

Stung, the forces of economic liberalism threw their energy
behind the 1896 presidential candidacy of reformer William
Jennings Bryan, in an effort to carry out a counterrevolution
through the electorate. Bryan's platform included measures
directed against the Court and its laissez-faire policies.
Nonetheless, the electoral effort failed. Bryan was defeated by
the conservative William McKinley. The outcome has been
described as follows:

> *The defeat of Bryan...was a great victory for
> American conservatism.... The judicial triumph of
> conservatism in the spring of 1895 had been confirmed
> by the political triumph of 1896. The conservative
> crisis of the 1890's was over.*[197]

In the aftermath of its 1895 conservative revolution, the
Court continued in an activist manner to fulfill its newly acquired role as judicial censor of economic reform legislation.[198]
Substantive due process - the centerpiece of constitutional
economic conservatism - took on its definitive form in the
1890's. The 1897 case, *Allgeyer v. Louisiana*,[199] was the first to
employ the fully mature substantive due process/liberty of contract doctrine to nullify a state economic reform statute.[200]

According to this doctrine, socio-economic legislation that
unreasonably restricts the liberty of individuals and corporations to make contracts and use their property as they see fit
denies the due process required by the Constitution's fifth and
fourteenth amendments. This same theory had been rejected,

---

196. 158 U.S. at 695 (on rehearing).

197. Paul, *Conservative Crisis*, at 226.

198. The conservatism of the Court in the 1890's was not limited to the area of economic
reform legislation. In the race relations area, for example, the Court continued its reactionary course by approving the "separate but equal" formula that nullified the equal protection clause and ratified the Jim Crow system of legally sanctioned segregation. *E.g.*,
Plessy v. Ferguson, 163 U.S. 537 (1896). Similarly, the Court was very conservative in
criminal procedure cases.

199. 165 U.S. 578 (1897).

200. The statute concerned out-of-state insurance sales.

over Justice Field's dissent, in the 1873 *Slaughterhouse Cases* on the ground that "due process" is concerned only with procedural regularity and not with the reasonableness of government action.[201] In the conservative climate of the 1890's, the Court reversed itself and adopted Field's proposition that the due process clauses impose substantive restraints on economic legislation.[202] During the remainder of its second conservative era, the Court was to use this interpretation of due process to strike down child labor laws, maximium hour/minimum wage regulations, legislation outlawing anti-labor "yellow dog" contracts, rate regulation of railroads and other corporate entities, as well as several major New Deal reforms.

While waging its war against economic reform, the Fuller Court availed itself of a number of powerful constitutional weapons in addition to substantive due processes. State economic reform laws were repeatedly invalidated on the grounds that they unreasonably burdened interstate commerce and thus violated the dormant commerce clause. Out of whole cloth, the Court invented the rule, later repudiated, that the Constitution's tenth amendment created a system of dual federalism in which enormous areas of legislative activity were exclusively reserved for the states and hence were immune from federal legislation. This theory was used in *E.C. Knight* as the basis for holding that Congress has no power to regulate manufacturing industries. The tenth amendment/dual federalism theory was also used to restrict other of Congress's legislative powers such as its prerogatives to tax and spend and to regulate agriculture, mining, and other so-called intrastate activities. Other constitutional provisions used to restrain economic reforms included the contract clause and the equal protection clause.

However, although the dominant theme of the 1890-1905 period of Supreme Court history was distinctly economic conservatism, it would be mistaken to conclude that liberal decisions were entirely absent from the Justices' holdings. On the

---

201. *See* pp. 73-74 *supra*.
202. *Cf.* Smyth v. Ames, 169 U.S. 466 (1898), another well known conservative decision holding that due process requires state railroad commissions to set rates high enough to allow a fair return on a fair valuation of the railroads' property, as determined according to a formula established by the Court itself.

contrary, just as the Taney Court had its conservative side, the Fuller Court had a liberal side too. Perhaps the most important expression of that liberalism was the emergence of a new, broad interpretation of the commerce power authorizing federal "police power" legislation in matters previously relegated to the states.

The leading case in this line was *Champion v. Ames*,[203] which held that congressional authority "to regulate Commerce with foreign Nations, and among the several States" included the power to exclude lottery tickets from interstate commerce. The power to exclude was considered plenary, and could be exercised to destroy commerce in undesired commodities as well as to protect commerce in desired commodities.

Similarly, many pieces of state economic reform legislation survived the test of constitutionality before the Court during this period. Indeed, some conservatives complained that the Court was not doing enough to stem the tide of socialism. Their concern was, for practical purposes, without cause. On the Fuller Court, liberalism was, without question, subordinate to the primary theme of conservative constitutional activism.

As the nineteenth century drew to a close, the hard line endorsed by the Court majority gradually began to soften. The severe depression that descended in 1893 eased in late 1897. By the following year, recovery was well underway and the start of a long period of relatively stable prosperity (1898-1914) was at hand. This brought a lessening of the social unrest that had, in turn, prompted the conservative backlash. "With the passing of the social and economic tensions of the mid-1890's the Court tended toward moderation in the use of its expanded powers."[204]

In addition, a series of relatively liberal appointments pushed the Bench into a more moderate posture. In 1897, the conservative Field retired. He was replaced by Joseph McKenna (1898-1925), who was a conservative at the start of his judicial career, developed into a moderate liberal, and then moved

203. 188 U.S. 321 (1903).
204. 3 Friedman & Israel, *The Justices of the United States*, at 1528.

back to the right late in his tenure[205]. In 1902, the moderate Horace Gray was succeeded by one of the giants of Supreme Court history, Oliver Wendell Holmes, Jr. (1902-32), a basically conservative individual who became a leading liberal Justice due to his deep commitment to judicial restraint.[206] The following year, the moderate conservative Shiras was replaced by William R. Day (1903-22), a moderate.[207] The following chart shows the closely balanced line-up after those three appointments:

TABLE K

Alignment of Justices - 1903-1906

Liberal	Moderate	Conservative
Harlan	White	Brewer
Holmes	Day	Peckham
McKenna	Brown	Fuller

Despite the gradual liberalization of the Justices and of public opinion in the nation at large, the Court's first age of laissez faire continued at least until 1905 when the most notorious substantive due process decision of all, *Lochner v. New York*,[208] was handed down. At issue was a New York statute limiting the working day of bakery employees to ten hours. For years, minimum wage/maximum hour legislation had been one of the most basic and consistent demands of the economic reform movement. At the same time, the question of wages and hours was considered by the conservatives to be at the heart of the "liberty of contract" granted exemption from governmental regulation.

---

205. Matthew McDevitt, *Joseph McKenna* (New York: Da Capo Press, 1946), *passim;* 3 Friedman & Israel, *The Justices of the United States*, at 1719-36.

206. Holmes is probably the second most famous and admired Justice in the history of the Court, ranking behind only John Marshall. He played a major role in the Court's liberal wing for many years and will be mentioned frequently in ensuing pages.

207. "To his credit, Day, in recognizing many of the vast social changes, adjusted his legal philosophy and became a moderate liberal in terms of favoring the extension of federal powers. Except for his stubborn reliance on Melville Fuller's odd definition of commerce, Justice Day generally cast his vote on the side of the twentieth century." 3 Friedman & Israel, *The Justices of the United States*, at 1788.

208. 198 U.S. 45 (1905).

In *Lochner*, the Court, by a narrow 5-4 margin, held the maximum hour statute to be an unconstitutional infringement of liberty of contract. The majority included, of course, the "three archconservatives,"[209] Peckham, who wrote the opinion, Brewer, and Fuller. Harlan, Holmes, Day, and White dissented. Had it not been for the defection of McKenna, the liberals would have prevailed. The *Lochner* case shows that the forces of laissez faire were still in control as late as 1905 but that the margin of dominance was growing very thin.

---

209. 3 Friedman & Israel, *The Justices of the United States*, at 1533.

Chapter Nine

The Not Quite Progressive Era (1906-1920)[210]

In the face of entrenched conservatism on the Supreme Court, the popular forces that during the late 1800's presented the rich with formidable challenges did not fold their tents and disappear into the night. On the contrary, the reformers swallowed hard and then simply continued their struggle in the best tradition of the Grangers, Populists, labor organizers, free silver inflationists, and suffragettes who were their political ancestors.

Early in the 1900's, the reform movement began to recover from the judicial setbacks of the 1890's and to register significant gains once again. After a short while, a coalition operating under the name of progressivism attained political ascendancy first within key state governments and then on a national scale. As happened with Jeffersonianism, however, progressivism never succeeded in gaining control of the Supreme Court. Rather, it was in the executive and legislative branches of government that the coalition's achievements were greatest.

---

210. As previously indicated, designation of the year 1906 as the start of the Court's "not quite progressive" era is somewhat arbitrary. *See* n. 167 *supra.* Clearly the Court moved from a reactionary posture in the 1890's to a more liberal posture in the years before and after 1910, but no clear cut boundary exists between the two periods. A case can be made for selecting the year 1910, when Charles Evan Hughes was seated, as the start of the "liberal interlude." Pfeffer, *This Honorable Court,* at 250-53. The choice of 1906 as the starting point is based primarily on the seating of William H. Moody, which brought the liberal wing back up to four Justices, and on the fact that liberal decisions began to appear in greater numbers in the 1906-10 period. Note also that 1906 was the year in which Charles Evans Hughes was elected Governor of New York on a reform platform.

The principle sources of the material presented in this chapter are the following: Croly, *The Promise of American Life;* Arthur S. Link, *Woodrow Wilson and the Progressive Era* (New York: Harper & Row, 1954); Alpheus T. Mason, *Brandeis, A Free Man's Life* (New York: The Viking Press, 1946); Pringle, *Theodore Roosevelt;* Arthur Schlesinger, Jr., *The Crisis of the Old Order* (Boston: Houghton Mifflin Co., 1957).

101

The progressives took effective control of the Democratic Party in 1896. From then until 1911, the party was for the most part dominated by "the Great Commoner," William Jennings Bryan, a thoroughgoing reformer and champion of the poor. Bryan, a former Nebraska congressman and prominent spokesman for the ill-fated 1894 income tax that was held unconstitutional in *Pollock*, was first nominated for the presidency by the Democrats in 1896 after his famous "You shall not crucify mankind upon a cross of gold" speech. Bryan was also the Democratic presidential candidate in 1900 and 1908. During this period (from 1896 to 1911), however, the Democrats were unable to win a presidential election.

The impulse for reform was so strong that it also began to make inroads within the Republican Party, which, since the 1870's, had been dominated by the interests of wealth and conservatism. To be sure, the Republicans continued to have stalwart conservative leaders such as President McKinley and Nelson Aldrich, the dominant voice of the Senate. But by the turn of the century, progressive Republican "insurgents" were making their presence felt. In 1900, for example, Robert M. La Follette was elected Governor of Wisconsin and promptly turned the state into a "laboratory of democracy."[211]

The Republican progressives received a major boost when McKinley was assassinated in 1901 and succeeded by Theodore Roosevelt, the fairweather reformer whose presidency lasted until 1909. Roosevelt's "Square Deal" programs included significant efforts to curb many of the excesses of the corporate rich. Among his most publicized measures were the stiff enforcement of antitrust laws ("trust busting") and the campaign for the conservation of natural resources. His tenure also saw the enactment of the Pure Food and Drug Act, the Federal Employers' Liability Act, the Hepburn Act, which restored the ICC's power to set railroad rates, and a variety of other economic reform statutes.

Roosevelt additionally made three rather liberal appointments to the Supreme Court. Following his success in getting the liberal Holmes and the moderate Day seated on the Bench,[212] he then selected his close friend and advisor William

---

211. Charles Sellers & Henry May, *A Synopsis of American History* (Chicago: Rand McNally & Co., 1963), at 284.

212. *See* p. 99 *supra*.

H. Moody (1906-10)[213] to succeed the moderate Brown. Said one commentator: "Moody's legal approach was careful and cautious but distinctly progressive in a liberal nationalistic sense."[214]

The following table delineates the line-up on the Court from Moody's appointment until 1909:

TABLE L

Alignment of Justices - 1906 to 1909

Liberal	Moderate	Conservative
Harlan	Day	Brewer
Holmes	White	Peckham
Moody		Fuller
McKenna		

Clearly, judicial liberalism had enjoyed a resurgence, although on economic issues the Court was very closely balanced and no faction was numerically strong enough to claim complete control. But a case can be made that Moody's appointment gave the liberals at least a slight edge for the first time since the early 1890's.

A well known decision indicative of the increased liberalism of the "Teddy Roosevelt Court" was that handed down in *Muller v. Oregon.*[215] At issue was an Oregon statute prohibiting the employment of women in factories and laundries for more than ten hours a day. Muller had been convicted of working his female laundry employees in excess of this limit, and he appealed the conviction claiming that the statute comprised an unreasonable interference with liberty of contract. The statute plainly touched upon the core area of the liberty of contract concept, hours of employment. The 1905 *Lochner v. New York*[216] decision, for example, had held un-

---

213. *See* 3 Friedman & Israel, *The Justices of the United States,* at 1801-21. While in the House of Representatives (1895-1902), Moody played a major role in pushing the Hepburn Act through Congress restoring the ICC's rate-setting powers which had been stripped by the Court. He was a trust-buster who also held "advanced" pro-labor views. At the time of his appointment, he was criticized as "too radical." *Id.* at 1815.

214. *Id.* at 1819.

215. 208 U.S. 412 (1908).

216. 198 U.S. 45 (1905); see pp. 99-100 *supra.*

constitutional a ten-hour work day statute for men and had made it clear that the Court was prepared to nullify wage and hour legislation it found to be unreasonable.

In order to rebut the claim that the Oregon statute comprised an unreasonable interference with the employer's liberty, Louis Dembitz Brandeis, the "people's lawyer" and later a Supreme Court Justice, submitted his landmark "Brandeis brief," a singular compilation that amassed the available sociological data underscoring the need for protective maximum hour legislation. Brandeis' reliance on empirical studies was a tactic new to the annals of judicial advocacy and introduced a helpful element of reality into the Court's analysis of rich-poor issues. In the *Muller* case, it played a major role in persuading the Justices to uphold the Oregon statute unanimously.

Such victories for economic liberalism were, however, matched during this period by equally impressive wins for the conservatives. In *Adair v. United States* (1908),[217] for example, a federal statute prohibiting anti-labor yellow dog contracts was held unconstitutional.[218] That same year, in *Loewe v. Lawlor*,[219] the Court held labor unions to be subject to the Sherman Antitrust Act, the 1890 measure prohibiting restraints of foreign and interstate trade, and affirmed a treble damage award against representatives of the United Hatters of North America for engaging in a boycott found to be illegal.

A decision that perfectly illustrated the Court's conservative/liberal split was the *First Employers' Liability Cases* (1908),[220] which held the 1906 Federal Employers' Liability Act unconstitutional because it purported to cover employees not involved in interstate commerce and therefore exceeded the power of Congress under the commerce clause. Justice White wrote the opinion for a five-vote majority that included the conservatives Brewer, Peckham, and Fuller, and the moderate Day. The Court's entire liberal wing dissented.

It was against this background of a closely balanced Supreme Court which supplied progressives with a few tangible judicial

---

217. 208 U.S. 161 (1908).
218. A yellow dog contract is an employment contract containing an agreement by the employee not to join a union.
219. 208 U.S. 274 (1908) (the so-called Danbury Hatters' case).
220. 207 U.S. 463 (1908).

gains without seriously jeopardizing the predominant position of entrenched conservative power that Roosevelt made a major mistake. While refusing all entreaties to seek a third presidential term, he placed his considerable influence solidly in support of William Howard Taft's bid for the nomination. Taft was essentially a conservative at heart, but in the 1908 election year he was temporarily caught in the grip of a progressive outlook. Professor Link describes Roosevelt's failure to perceive Taft's true political nature as follows:

> His one great mistake, and it was an error of personal judgement, was in choosing William Howard Taft to succeed him. If Roosevelt had selected Charles Evans Hughes, the brilliant, crusading, and independent Governor of New York, the future history of the United States might have been considerably different.[221]

After his nomination and election, Taft lost little time in aligning himself with the Republican Party's conservative Old Guard and against the Party's progressive "insurgents." In the 1910 off-year congressional elections, for example, he helped orchestrate a general attempt to defeat midwest progressive Republicans. To quote Link again:

> In order to prevent the disruption of the Republican party, Taft had to facilitate the shift in party control from the Old Guard to the insurgents. Instead of boldly doing this, he vacillated at first, finally aligned himself with the reactionaries, and so completely alienated the progressives that a rupture was inevitable.[222]

Ironically, the golden opportunity to reduce the influence of laissez faire on the Supreme Court and inaugurate a new phase of economic liberalism came in 1909 and 1910 when all three of the Bench's arch-conservatives, Brewer, Peckham, and Fuller, died. With the progressive movement then gaining

---

221. Link, *Woodrow Wilson and the Progressive Era*, at 3.
222. *Id.*

momentum on a national scale, had Taft remained in the mold that had sparked so much enthusiasm on his predecessor's part, the liberals could easily have picked up the fifth vote needed to assure their primacy on the Court.[223] It was at this point, however, that Roosevelt's mistake made itself felt, for precisely at this time Taft moved sharply to the right politically.

Because of the additional retirement of Moody in 1910 and the death of Harlan in 1911, Taft had five seats to fill and thus an opportunity to create a 7-2 majority for the liberals. Instead, his choices were four moderates and conservatives, Horace Lurton (1910-14), Willis Van Devanter (1911-37), Joseph Lamar (1911-16), and Mahlon Pitney (1912-22), and only one liberal, Charles Evans Hughes (1910-16).[224] As a result, the liberal bloc was actually reduced from four to three.

The following table shows the general line-up on the Court after Taft's five appointees were seated:

TABLE M

Alignment of Justices - 1911 to 1914

Liberal	Moderate	Conservative
Holmes	White	Van Devanter
Hughes	Lurton	Lamar
McKenna	Pitney	
	Day	

223. Actually, for a brief time after the appointment of Charles Evans Hughes (1910-16), the Court did have a five-vote liberal majority (Harlan, Holmes, Hughes, Moody, and McKenna). Moody, however, had already become partially disabled by the rheumatism that forced his retirement in 1910 and left him crippled, and Harlan died within the year. So the moment was fleeting.

224. Horace Lurton (1910-14) was a jurist of "ingrained conservatism" who had a "general conservative approach" to legal questions. 3 Friedman & Israel, *The Justices of the United States*, at 1855. At the time of his appointment, protests were raised because of Lurton's alleged "favoritism" toward corporations and property rights, and Samuel Gompers labelled him a "narrow conservative." *Id.* at 1888. During his brief term on the Court, Lurton was a moderate.

Willis Van Devanter (1911-37) was a conservative who, after a somewhat moderate first few years, became a stalwart of the Court's right wing. "[H]e was the most intractable of the reactionary justices of the 1930's." *Id.* at 1952. Harlan Fiske Stone later described him as "the commander-in-chief of the judicial reaction." *Id.*

Joseph R. Lamar (1911-16) was a "cautious, temperate, and conservative" Justice who "accepted the predominant conservative ideas of his era." *Id.* at 1988.

In spite of the opportunity lost for a truly progressive Court, Taft's appointments did not appreciably alter the somewhat more liberal viewpoints that had characterized the Court since 1906. A combination of factors contributed to the continuity of this balance. First, the new conservatives were far less extreme in their thinking than men like Field, Brewer, and Peckham. Second, the liberal Charles Evans Hughes seems to have exerted an influence over his peers in excess of his one vote in nine. Third, and most important, the Court was affected by the increasingly progressive climate of public opinion throughout the nation.

In 1910, the progressive movement achieved its greatest political victory to date. Within the Republican Party, the struggle between progressives and conservatives for control reached a climax in the spring of that year. When Taft aligned himself with the conservatives, the progressives turned to the idea of a third-party movement under the leadership of Theodore Roosevelt.

The net result of Taft's shift to the right, and the ensuing split in the Republican ranks, was a democratic victory in the 1910 off-year elections. For the first time since 1892, Democrats took control of the House of Representatives. Moreover, progressive candidates swept into power in a number of key states. For example, Woodrow Wilson captured New Jersey's governorship and Hiram Johnson overthrew the dominance of the Southern Pacific to become California's governor. Both Wilson and Johnson inaugurated highly successful economic reform programs within their respective states.

Progressive ascendency in the federal government came with the election of 1912. By then, the split within the Republican Party had become irreconcilable. When the pro-Taft forces

---

Mahlon Pitney (1912-22) was a "conservative of the Taft stripe." Alpheus T. Mason, *The Supreme Court from Taft to Warren* (New York: W.W. Norton & Co., 1958), at 54. His appointment was opposed by the progressives. On the Court, he stook a strongly anti-labor, anti-civil liberties position and helped fulfill "Taft's expectations...(that) the Court would act as the great bulwark against radical innovations." 3 Friedman & Israel, *The Justices of the United States*, at 2001.

Charles Evans Hughes (1910-16, 1930-41), on the other hand, was "one of the outstanding liberal members of the Court during his initial period of service." *Id.* at 1901. Later in his career, Hughes' "essentially conservative cast of mind" pushed him into a more moderate position." *Id.* at 1914.

steamrollered the Republican nominating convention, Theodore Roosevelt and his faction walked out. On August 6, 1912, the Progressive, or Bull Moose, Party was formed. The new party not unexpectedly selected as its presidential candidate Theodore Roosevelt, who was at this point an enthusiastic progressive.

Enthusiasm notwithstanding, in the November election, Taft and Roosevelt split the Republican vote, allowing Woodrow Wilson to achieve a plurality victory. At the same time, the Democrats retained their control of the House of Representatives and captured the Senate as well. Wilson, personally an interesting mix of conservatism and progressivism, had run on a strongly progressive platform. Thus, the election amounted to a glorious victory for the advocates of economic reform.[225]

Wilson's 1913 inauguration was followed by a period of legislation enacted in keeping with his progressive platform. In rapid succession, statutes were passed reducing the protective tariffs that had sheltered big business for years, regulating the banking system that had been dominated by the House of Morgan, the Rockefeller Group (including Kuhn, Loeb & Co.), and other financial powers then popularly known as the "money trust") and imposing a graduated income tax.[226] Simultaneously, progressive measures continued to flow out of state legislatures as well.

Naturally, the progressive economic reforms were promptly challenged in the courts. "The hot controversy of the day," legal historian Merlo J. Pusey has stated, "was over the extent to which 'freedom of contract' restrained the states from passing social legislation."[227] In a substantial number of these challenges, the advocates of social and economic reform legislation prevailed. Thus, to cite two instances, the Court unanimously upheld a 10-hour work day for women statute in

---

225. The extent of the progressive mood within the country is made clear by the fact that both liberals, Wilson and Roosevelt, ran well ahead of the conservative Taft. In fact, the real contest was between the liberal Democrats and the Progressives, with the Republicans pretty much conceding long before the election.

226. The sixteenth amendment had been ratified in 1913 removing the obstacle created by the *Pollock* case.

227. Merlo J. Pusey, *Charles Evans Hughes* (New York: The Macmillan Co., 1961), at 310.

Riley v. Massachusetts (1914)[228] and an 8-hour day, 48-hour work week for women statute in Miller v. Wilson (1915).[229] The Bench's relative tolerance of progressive legislative measures also was illustrated by Justice Hughes' opinion in Chicago, B.&O. Ry. Co. v. McGuire (1911)[229] upholding a state law that outlawed employment contracts which required employees to waive their right to sue for damages caused by industrial accidents. Hughes wrote:

> Freedom of contract is a qualified and not an absolute right. There is no absolute freedom to do as one wills or contract as one chooses. The guaranty of liberty does not withdraw from legislative supervision that wide department of activity which consists of the making of contracts or deny to government the power to provide restrictive safeguards. Liberty implies the absence of arbitrary restraint, not immunity from reasonable regulations and prohibitions imposed in the interests of the community.[230]

The Court's conservative side continued, however, to assert itself at crucial moments. Perhaps the most striking example of the remaining power of laissez faire concepts among the Justices was Coppage v. Kansas (1915),[231] which struck down a state statute outlawing yellow dog contracts, thus making the doctrine of Adair v. United States applicable to state as well as federal legislation.[232]

In 1916, Justice Hughes resigned from the Court to become the Republican presidential candidate. The Wilson Administration, after a lapse into conservative postures during 1914 and 1915, responded to Hughes' challenge with a second burst of progressive legislation. Statutes were enacted providing guaranteed loans to farmers, establishing a workmen's compensation system, prohibiting the interstate transportation of goods produced by child labor, and providing for increas-

---

228. 232 U.S. 671 (1914).
229. 236 U.S. 373 (1915).
230. 219 U.S. 549, 567 (1911).
231. 236 U.S. 1 (1915).
232. Cf. notes 217, 218 supra.

ed self-government for the Philippine Islands. By the close of 1916, the Wilsonian Democrats had taken essentially their entire platform of 1912 and transformed it into law.[233]

What was the Supreme Court's reaction to this unprecedented burst of reform activity? There can be little doubt that much of the Wilsonian legislative program would have been declared unconstitutional by the Supreme Court of the 1890's. By 1916, the appointive process had resulted in a Court whose members were much more flexible in their thinking as to what economic regulations were permissable under the Constitution. Nevertheless, despite the Court's general liberalization, the power of the conservatives was not definitively broken, and the judicial doctrines of laissez faire continued to pose a threat to economic reform programs.

Although Wilson made only three Supreme Court appointments during his two-term presidency, he had the opportunity to create a five-vote liberal majority on the Bench if he had chosen his Justices wisely. He irrevocably lost his chance, however, when he selected James C. McReynolds (1914-41) to replace Horace Lurton. McReynolds, who had achieved a reputation as a liberal because of his work on Justice Department antitrust litigation, actually turned out to be one of the most reactionary Justices ever to sit on the highest Court in the land.[234]

From the perspective of progressivism, Wilson did much better with his next two nominations. In 1916, along with Hughes' resignation, Joseph R. Lamar died. Wilson, at the time, was in a mood of advanced domestic progressivism and selected two well-known liberals to fill the openings. The first was Louis Dembitz Brandeis (1916-38), who has aptly been described as "the first thoroughgoing progressive ever to be appointed to the Supreme Court."[235] The second was John H. Clarke (1916-22), who was "known for his liberal views" and

---

233. Link, *Woodrow Wilson and the Progressive Era*, at 223 *et seq.*

234. A strong case can be made for the proposition that McReynolds is number one in the ranks of reactionary Supreme Court Justices ahead of even Field, Brewer, and the early Federalists. McReynolds was "the Court's staunchest defender of due process in protecting the rights of businessmen." 3 Friedman & Israel, *The Justices of the United States*, at 2030. "Of the four conservative Justices famous for their opposition to Franklin Roosevelt's New Deal, James Clark McReynolds was probably the most reactionary and easily the most tenacious." *Id.* at 2023.

235. Mason, *Brandeis, A Free Man's Life*, at 514.

who wrote to Brandeis, "I am looking forward with unusual confidence to pleasant association with you because of what I suppose is something of a community point of view between us."[236] It is clear that Wilson hoped Brandeis and Clarke would combat the anti-progressive views that still remained on the Court:

> *Like thousands of other liberals throughout the country [Wilson later stated in a letter to Justice Clarke] I have been counting on the influence of you and Justice Brandeis to restrain the Court in some measure from the extreme reactionary course which it seems inclined to follow.*[237]

With the seating of Brandeis and Clarke in 1916, the balance of power on the Court looked like this:

TABLE N

Alignment of Justices - 1916 to 1920

Liberal	Moderate	Conservative
Brandeis	White	McReynolds
Holmes	Pitney	Van Devanter
C l a r k e	D a y	
McKenna		

At this juncture, the seriousness of Wilson's error in appointing McReynolds became clear. McReynolds, by aligning himself with Taft's two remaining appointees, Van Devanter and Pitney, and the moderates White and Day, deprived liberalism of the fifth vote it needed to gain control of the Bench. The result was that the reign of laissez faire remained unbroken.

---

236. *Id.* at 513. It has been speculated that Brandeis, who had been Wilson's intimate friend and advisor for years, recommended the appointment of Clarke. Clarke was "fairly far to the left within the limits of sound progressivism, and was prepared to back up a broad extension of state and national power." 3 Friedman & Israel, *The Justices of the United States*, at 2081. Clarke also showed "particular generosity toward labor." *Id.* at 2083. At the time of his resignation in 1922, the New York *Globe* wrote, "He is a liberal among conservatives, and he was needed." *Id.* at 2085.

237. Quoted in Jackson, *The Struggle for Judicial Supremacy*, at 186.

Hammer v. Dagenhart (1918)[238] vividly illustrates the inability of the Court's liberal plurality to bring about an era of judicial progressivism. For many years, one of the reform movement's most consistent demands had been for the abolition of child labor practices by which young children, due to the extreme poverty suffered by their parents, were forced to work long hours under frequently terrible working conditions. The advocates of laissez faire resisted these entreaties on the ground that such legislation would be "paternalistic" and would interfere with liberty of contract.

In 1916, the Wilson Administration finally succeeded in obtaining the enactment of a federal statute prohibiting the interstate shipment of goods manufactured by means of child labor. The legislation was quickly challenged. When it arrived before the Supreme Court in *Hammer*, the law was declared unconstitutional in a 5-4 decision. Writing for the majority, Justice Day, in the best tradition of laissez faire conservatism, concluded that the real purpose of the statute was to regulate manufacturing and that the Constitution's commerce clause does not give Congress the power to regulate manufacturing as opposed to transportation. Holmes, Brandeis, Clarke, and McKenna dissented futilely.[239]

Since the concurrence of only one of the Bench's three moderate Justices was needed to give the liberals a majority in any case, the progressives continued to enjoy occasional triumphs. A leading example is *Bunting v. Oregon* (1917),[240] which, without mentioning it, overruled the 1905 *Lochner* decision and upheld a general 10-hour work day statute.[241] McKenna, whose defection had provided the fifth vote for the conservatives in *Lochner*, recanted, returned to the liberal fold, and wrote the majority opinion upholding the legislation, with the support of Holmes, Clarke, Day, and Pitney. Brandeis did not participate.

---

238. 247 U.S. 251 (1918).

239. Other illustrative conservative victories included Hitchman Coal & Coke Co. v. Mitchell, 245 U.S. 229 (1918), which upheld injunctions restraining unions from soliciting employees who had signed yellow dog contracts, and Adams v. Tanner, 244 U.S. 590 (1917), which held unconstitutional a state law prohibiting employment agency fees.

240. 243 U.S. 426 (1917).

241. *Cf.* Wilson v. New, 243 U.S. 332 (1917), which upheld the Adamson Act maximum hour and minimum wage provisions covering employees of interstate carriers.

But even these small advances of liberalism were to prove short-lived. For, after almost 15 years of rulings that dispensed substantial gains and losses to liberals and conservatives alike, the prevailing mood of the Court's second conservative era was about to reassert itself, and laissez faire was soon to hold sway once again.

Chapter Ten

The Second Age of
Laissez Faire (1921-1937)[242]

A. The 1920's and the Taft Court

*In 1920 the Supreme Court was still what Marshall
had conceived it to be - the protector and guardian of
property. And that was to be its role during the decade
in which William Howard Taft was Chief Justice.*[243]

The presidential election of 1920 can be viewed as a national
referendum in which progressive government was overwhelmingly rejected. The nation was tired of reform politics. A record
seven million vote landslide in favor of the conservative
Republican Warren G. Harding resoundingly demonstrated
that the nation's people wanted to return to "business as
usual." The federal government, having grown fat and powerful during World War I, was to be cut back and the business of
the nation put into the hands of the free enterprise system.

Former President William Howard Taft, a fervent Harding
supporter, worked industriously during the 1920 presidential
campaign to make the Supreme Court a major election issue.
Taft realized that the Court would have at least four vacancies
during the early 1920's and that its future political posture
would depend upon whether conservatives or liberals were
selected for those seats.

---

242. The principle sources of the material presented in this chapter are the following:
Jackson, *The Struggle for Judicial Supremacy;* Mason, *The Supreme Court from Taft to
Warren,* and Schlesinger, *The Crisis of the Old Order.*
243. Pfeffer, *This Honorable Court,* at 269.

Of all Taft's deeds during his presidency, he was perhaps proudest of his conservative appointments to the Court. He was also keenly aware of the manner in which these Justices had used their judicial prerogatives to protect propertied interests against the proponents of progressive reform.[244] Now that his appointees were about to leave the Bench, Taft was determined to secure replacements who would carry on in the conservative tradition and maintain the judiciary as the final bulwark in the defense of property.[245] Taft's most famous statement during the campaign on this issue was the following:

> *Mr. Wilson is in favor of a latitudinarian construction of the Constitution of the United States to weaken the protection it should afford against socialistic raids upon property rights....He has made three appointments to the Supreme Court. He is understood to be greatly disappointed in the attitude of the first of these [McReynolds] upon such questions. The other two [Brandeis and Clarke] represent a new school of constitutional construction, which if allowed to prevail, will greatly impair our fundamental law. Four of the incumbent Justices are beyond the retiring age of seventy, and the next President will probably be called upon to appoint their successors. There is no greater domestic issue in this election than the maintenance of the Supreme Court as the bulwark to enforce the guaranty that no man shall be deprived of his property without the process of law.*[246]

The Harding landslide of 1920 gave Taft exactly what he wanted. In the years following Harding's inauguration, vacancies on the Court came swiftly and the empty seats were filled exclusively by conservatives. The first of these was Taft

---

244. Taft's biographer stated, "Above all other things he was proudest of the fact that six of the nine members of the Supreme Court bore his commission. 'And I have said to them,' Taft chuckled, 'Damn you, if any of you die, I'll disown you.' " 2 Pringle, *The Life And Times of William Howard Taft* (New York: Farrar & Rinehart, Inc., 1939), at 854.

245. On the side, Taft may also have hoped that he would be one of the conservatives chosen if Harding was elected. He was.

246. Quoted in Mason, *The Supreme Court from Taft to Warren*, at 40.

himself (1921-30),[247] who replaced the deceased moderate-conservative Chief Justice White. Taft's attitude toward organized labor, around which major judicial issues frequently arose, is illustrative of his prejudices against the poor in general. On this subject, in a 1922 letter to his brother, he wrote:

> The only class which is distinctly arrayed against the Court is a class that does not like the courts at any rate, and that is organized labor. That faction we have to hit every little while, because they are continually violating the law and depending on threats and violence to accomplish their purpose.[248]

In 1922, Clarke retired, to be replaced by George Sutherland (1922-38). Sutherland, a conservative Republican from Utah, "had served in the Senate from 1905 to 1917, where he consistently opposed the progressive policies of Roosevelt and Wilson."[249] He was later to become the "intellectual spokesman" of the four-vote conservative bloc of the 1930's. The Clarke/Sutherland succession marked a substantial shift to the right, as it represented the loss of a liberal as well as the addition of a conservative. That same year, the moderate William R. Day retired. His seat was filled by Pierce Butler (1923-39), a successful railroad attorney from Minnesota and an extreme conservative.[251] Finally, in 1923, the moderate-conservative Pitney retired and was succeeded by Edward Sanford (1923-30), another moderate-conservative.

Thus, by the time Harding's reshaping of the Court was complete, the Justices were overall as Taft had hoped: extremely conservative on economic issues and fully armed to strike

---

247. "Taft was a thoroughgoing Social Darwinist, stubborn defender of the *status quo*, apologist for economic privilege, inveterate critic of social democracy - the gigantic symbol of stand-pattism." 3 Friedman & Israel, *The Justices of the United States*, at 2104. "His enduring aim...(was) to safeguard private property. Courts were (in Taft's opinion) America's primary reliance for preserving this bulwark of civilization." *Id.* at 2103.

248. Pfeffer, *This Honorable Court*, at 274.

249. *Id.* at 271.

250. 3 Friedman & Israel, *The Justices of the United States*, at 2133.

251. "Butler's decisions throughout his years on the Court reveal an almost unrelenting conservatism." 3 Friedman & Israel, *The Justices of the United States*, at 2187. "Butler was among the most rigid of the justices who rejected New Deal legislation. His philosophy was that of laissez faire...." *Id.* at 2190.

down any more "socialistic raids" on property rights. As indicated in the following table, for the first time since the pre-Jacksonian period, the Bench had six tried and true conservatives, and its liberal wing was reduced to practical impotence.[252]

TABLE O

Alignment of Justices - 1923 to 1925

Liberal	Moderate	Conservative
Brandeis	McKenna	McReynolds
Holmes		Butler
		Sutherland
		Van Devanter
		Taft
		Sanford

With regard to this alignment, legal historian Alpheus Thomas Mason has stated:

> *As Taft had foreseen, reconstitution of the supreme bench quickly followed on the heels of Harding's election. By 1923 four of the nine Justices - George Sutherland, Pierce Butler, Edward Sanford and Taft himself as Chief Justice - had been appointed by the Republican President. With Willis Van Devanter, James McReynolds, and the infirm Joseph McKenna (succeeded in 1925 by Harlan Stone) these four judges - all staunchly conservative - heightened the rigidities of constitutional interpretation. The genial Chief Justice, described by his biograher as 'conservative, if not reactionary,' had now realized his long-cherished*

252. The 6-3 conservative majority remained unchanged until 1930. The only new Justice appointed between 1922 and 1930 was Harlan Fiske Stone (1925-46), who replaced Joseph McKenna. Since both Stone and McKenna were relatively liberal, no change was effected in the Court's line-up. Left to his own choice, President Coolidge would probably have chosen a conservative to replace McKenna. At that time, however, Coolidge was forced to go against his natural inclinations in order to placate the opposition aroused by the corrupt Harding administration.

ambition to preside over a court that could be counted on to quell any 'socialistic raids on property rights.' Soon after his appointment the Chief Justice (consistent with his view in shaping the law) announced at a conference of the Justices that he 'had been appointed to reverse a few decisions' and, with his famous chuckle, added, 'I looked right at old Holmes when I said it.'[253]

Harding's fulfillment of Taft's aspirations brought the Court's second age of laissez faire conservatism in with a vengeance. Once again, the majority assumed the task of "censoring" economic legislation and of nullifying legislative efforts on behalf of the poor to regulate and restrict the operation of the free enterprise system.[254]

The case which, above all others, provides a symbol for this renewed surge of judicial conservatism is *Adkins v. Children's Hospital* (1923).[255] At issue was the constitutionality of a minimum wage statute for women and children, exactly the type of legislation that had long been one of the most fundamental demands of progressivism. In deciding *Adkins*, the Court turned the clock back to 1905 and flatly held minimum wage legislation to be an unconstitutional infringement of the liberty of employers and employees to negotiate employment contracts. Justice Sutherland based his opinion for the Court squarely on *Lochner*. Freedom of contract, he wrote, is "the general rule and restraint the exception." From the standpoint of liberals and reformers, a new dark age had begun.[256]

Ironically, just when the Court emerged in full battle gear to defend the honor of laissez faire capitalism, its services became largely unnecessary. The progressive tide receded after 1916, and the nation emerged from World War I in an extremely conservative mood. The hallmarks of the immediate post-war

---

253. Mason, *The Supreme Court from Taft to Warren*, at 50.

254. *See, e.g.,* Bailey v. Drexel Furniture Co., 259 U.S. 20 (1922), which held the child labor tax of 1919 unconstitutional; Truax V. Corrigan, 257 U.S. 312 (1921), which held an Arizona statute restricting labor injunctions unconstitutional; Duplex Printing Press Co., v. Deering, 254 U.S. 443 (1921), which restricted the anti-injunction provisions of the Clayton Act.

255. 261 U.S. 525 (1923).

256. Taft dissented. Holmes joined him. Brandeis did not participate.

period were anti-subversive witchhunting, racial persecution, America-first isolationism, and economic conservatism. The 1920's were, *par excellence*, the decade of big business. As historian Mason has put it:

> To the loud acclaim of the business world, Harding sounded the keynote of the next decade of Republicanism: 'We want less government in business and more business in government.' The change was high-lighted by placing Andrew Mellon, number one businessman, monopolist, and multi-millionaire, at the head of the Treasury Department. The Republican party resigned leadership and practically gave over the government to business....[257]

During this period, businessmen emerged as heroes of popular culture. They dominated government. The prevailing belief was, "What's good for business is good for the country." In such a political climate, efforts to regulate business in the public interest were normally defeated by legislatures, and the services of the Court as the guardian of laissez faire were largely unneeded.[258]

Nevertheless, the Taft Court took advantage of opportunity when it arose and nullified twice as many economic regulations as had the Court of the 1910-20 period.[259] Central to this course on which the judicial majority embarked was a conservative attack on the important "property clothed with a public interest" doctrine that had been in effect since the landmark 1877 Chicago grain elevator ruling handed down in *Munn v. Illinois*.[260]

In *Munn*, the majority held that government possesses the general power necessary to regulate prices in businesses affected with a public interest. Moreover, *Munn* adopted a liberal, pragmatic approach to the issue, allowing regulation wherever business had some demonstrable impact on the public. The idea that most businesses have some demonstrable

---

257. Mason, *Brandeis, A Free Man's Life*, at 530.
258. The prestige of business was immensely strengthened by the tremendous economic boom that occurred from 1923 through 1928.
259. McCloskey, *The American Supreme Court*, at 158.
260. 97 U.S. 113 (1877); *see* pp. 75-76 *supra*.

effect on the public, and are therefore subject to price regulation, was to remain essentially intact until the 1920's.

Near the end of that decade, however, the Taft Court carried out a conservative counterrevolution in this area of law. Only a very few businesses such as railroads and public utilities, the Court ruled, are affected with sufficient public interest to warrant regulation. Other entities, including ticket brokers,[261] employment agencies,[262] and the vast majority of all business enterprises, were hence exempt from price regulation. In short, by merely redefining the terminology of "property clothed with a public interest," the Taft Court discarded the traditional rule permitting, in most instances, price and rate regulations and instituted a new rule banning such measures, in most instances.

The Court liberals, after a period of quiescence, challenged these actions vigorously. During the first half of the 1920's, they had yielded to Taft's pleas for solidarity and muted their voice of dissent and protest. As the decade progressed, however, the good feelings faded. When the country's economic boom started to wind down and hard times approached, the liberal bloc increasingly contested the majority's conservative doctrines. The conservative Justices, and Taft in particular, fearing a resurgence of popular radicalism, moved even farther to the right and increased their stridency. As a result, the Court of the late 1920's polarized into two hostile wings: Taft, McReynolds, Butler, Sutherland, Van Devanter, and Sanford on the right; Holmes, Brandeis, and Stone on the left. Here is Mason's description of the conservative camp's outlook at the time:

> *The line drawn between the conservative Right, led by the Chief Justice, and the liberal Left, consisting of Holmes, Brandeis, and Stone, became increasingly sharp....*
>
> *As his [Taft's] regime neared its end, he grew firm in the belief that the Court must hold the line; it must protect the sacred institutions of property and contract from troublemakers who stimulate popular pas-*

---

261. Tyson v. Banton, 273 U.S. 416 (1927).
262. Ribnik v. McBride, 277 U.S. 350 (1928).

sion and threaten encroachment. Outsiders, even though they be lawyers, who opposed the 'sound,' 'legal' way or suggested new lines of development - experimentation - were 'a lot of sentimentalists,' 'socialists,' 'progressives,' 'bolshevists.'

The Chief Justice was alarmed by Dean Roscoe Pound* and his sociological jurisprudence. Charles A. Beard, known for his economic interpretation of the Constitution, was brushed off as outstanding among 'all the fools I have run across.' Brandeis was denounced as 'a muckraker, an emotionalist for his own purposes, a Socialist...a man of much power for evil.' President Wilson's 'domestic program was far too radical.' Even Charles Evans Hughes was suspected of entertaining 'a few progressive notions.' In contrast, Andrew Mellon was praised as 'a long-headed financier,' and President Harding extolled for having 'on the whole done remarkably well.'

Under Taft's leadership, the majority envisioned itself in the van of national progress. The laissez-faire dogma, glorified in the writings of Adam Smith and Herbert Spencer, was the principal avenue to wealth and power. A minimum of lawmaking was raised to the level of an ideal.[263]

The Court's growing polarization was hardened further by the advent of depression in 1929. In the face of a deteriorating economy, the legal and popular sentiments enveloping the Court changed drastically. As in the 1890's, the people increasingly demanded that government take action to ease the financial crisis. Yet, the judicial doctrines developed in the 1920's were for the most part inconsistent with the kind of government action demanded. In short, the indications were that the Supreme Court was headed for a serious clash with the nation's legislative and executive institutions.

B. The 1930's and the Hughes Court

After the 1929 stock market collapse, the nation sank into

---

* Dean of Harvard Law School and leader of the legal realism movement.
263. Mason, *The Supreme Court from Taft to Warren*, at 61, 64.

the Great Depression. To the dismay of Chief Justice Taft, even President Herbert Hoover broke with traditional laissez faire policies and attempted, at least on a small scale, to cure the economy by government intervention. But the cure did not take. Inexorably, the depression deepened, in 1930, then 1931, then 1932. Demands for massive government action began to bear fruit, first at the state level, then at the federal level as well. But would the Court set aside its conservative, pro-laissez faire views and place the imprimatur of constitutionality on the new economic experiments?

In 1930, two changes in Court personnel created some hope among liberals that the Court would pull back from its rigid conservatism and permit the government to deal with the worsening depression. First, the reactionary Chief Justice Taft died, and Hoover chose Charles Evans Hughes (1910-16; 1930-41) to replace him. Liberals, recalling Hughes' earlier performance as reform governor of New York (1906-10) and as Associate Justice of the Supreme Court, and hoping that his subsequent corporate law practice had not destroyed his reforming propensities, had some reason to believe that Hughes would side with the liberal bloc. Second, the conservative Edward Sanford retired and was replaced by Owen Roberts (1930-45), a former special prosecutor of participants in the Teapot Dome oil scandal. Roberts, a Philadelphia attorney, admittedly looked rather conservative,[264] but the possibility was present that he would provide the fifth vote needed to allow legislatures and executive officers to act.

The two personnel changes of 1930 moved the Court from a solid 6-3 conservative majority to a more ambiguous 4-2-3 split with four conservatives (Sutherland, Butler, Van Devanter, and McReynolds), three liberals, (Holmes, Brandeis, and Stone), and two possible swing votes (Hughes and Roberts). Pfeffer offers this analysis of the 1930 Court:

Hughes's first entry to the Supreme Court in 1910 inaugurated a period of comparative liberalism, and his

---

264. In 1923, for example, Roberts had given a speech at a bankers' association meeting attacking the "encroachment of government in American life." 3 Friedman & Israel, *The Justices of the United States*, at 255. Although his early voting record showed some moderation, Roberts was a conservative during most of his tenure. His "very last years on the Court reveal a growing conservatism." *Id.* at 2262. At the end he was an "archaic fixture" on the Court. *Id.* at 2263.

*re-entry in 1930 appeared to be the harbinger of
another revival of liberalism. On the right, the
Praetorian Guard of laissez faire capitalism -
McReynolds, Van Devanter, Sutherland and Butler -
were as stalwart and as uncompromising as ever. On
the left, so too were the avante garde of Brandeis,
Stone and Holmes-Cardozo.* In the center were
Roberts and Hughes, the former perhaps slightly more
conservative than Sanford, but the latter far more
liberal than Taft. There appeared to be good reason for
liberals and progressives to be moderately optimistic
as to the future course of the Court.*[265]

In the 1932 presidential election, the American people
reversed their anti-reformist verdict of 1920. Twelve years of
"business as usual" in the private sector and "hands off the
economy" on the part of the government had resulted in an unprecedented national financial collapse rather than permanent
prosperity. Furthermore, when the business "experts" were
asked what to do about combatting the depression, they simply
did not know.[266] So the electorate turned to Franklin Delano
Roosevelt and his promise of vigorous federal response to the
severity of the times.

Immediately after his March 1933 inauguration, Roosevelt
redeemed his promise by generating a whirlwind legislative
program involving unprecedented federal intervention in the
economy. The "100 days" produced even more progressive
legislation than the Wilson administration had been responsible for in 1916. In short order, statutes were passed
regulating manufacturing (the National Industrial Recovery
Act), agriculture (the Agricultural Adjustment Act), the stock
market (the Securities Act), banking (the Emergency Banking
Act), and other parts of the economy's private sector. Having
passed muster in the White House and the Congress,
Roosevelt's New Deal now faced the stern test of judicial
review.

---

* Holmes retired in 1932. His replacement, Benjamin Nathan Cardozo (1932-38), one of
the most respected and beloved Justices in American legal history, was even more liberal
than Holmes. Thus, the 4-2-3 split was unchanged. Apart from Cardozo's appointment,
there were no personnel changes until 1937.

265. Pfeffer, *This Honorable Court*, at 291.
266. Schlesinger, *The Crisis of The Old Order*, at 457.

In his book, *The Struggle for Judicial Supremacy*, Robert H. Jackson, first the United States Solicitor General who personally briefed and argued the constitutionality of the New Deal before the Supreme Court and later an Associate Justice of the Court, notes that: "It was not until 1934 that cases involving governmental power to deal with depression problems caused the Court to speak."[267] Initially, when it did speak, the Court provided some encouragement for the New Dealers. In *Home Bldg. & Loan Ass'n. v. Blaisdell* (1934),[268] a majority opinion written by Chief Justice Hughes upheld a Minnesota statute declaring an emergency moratorium on mortgage foreclosures.[269] Shortly thereafter, Justice Roberts wrote the majority opinion in *Nebbia v. New York* (1934)[270] upholding a statute authorising the New York government to regulate milk prices.

Here was hope. Hughes and Roberts, the two new potential swing men, had sided with the reliable liberals Brandeis, Stone, and Cardozo in sustaining the power of government to deal with the hard times. Ominously, however, the Court's conservative Justices, who eventually acquired the moniker "the four horsemen," were dissenting as a bloc. Said Jackson:

> *Four of the Justices, Van Devanter, Sutherland McReynolds, and Butler, within one of a majority, were asserting a power and duty in the judiciary to stop any governing body - state or federal - from interfering with an economy of laissez faire.*[271]

Obviously, if either Hughes or Roberts faltered, the New Deal was in trouble.

And they did falter. In 1935, the tenuous liberal-moderate coalition disintegrated, and the Supreme Court began to void the New Deal by declaring many of its key federal statutory underpinnings unconstitutional.[272] Justice Roberts moved

---

267. Jackson, *The Struggle for Judicial Supremacy*, at 78.
268. 290 U.S. 398 (1934).
269. Protection against foreclosure on debts during hard times had, of course, been a consistent recommendation of reformers since the days of Shays' Rebellion.
270. 291 U.S. 502 (1934).
271. Jackson, *The Struggle for Judicial Supremacy*, at 82.
272. *Id.* at 86-123.

sharply to the right into close alignment with the four horsemen. Chief Justice Hughes additionally joined the conservatives in about half of the subsequent closely divided rulings. In fact, in a few instances, even the liberals, too, banded together with their conservative counterparts in nullifying New Deal legislation. But by far, the worst damage to Roosevelt's economic recovery programs was done by Roberts and the four horsemen, often over bloc dissents by the Court's liberal wing.

The string of cases involving constitutional challenges to New Deal legislation in the 1935-36 period is long and fascinating. At the outset came *Panama Refining Co. v. Ryan* (1935),[273] overturning a federal statute designed to regulate the petroleum industry. An early exception to the Court's emerging pattern of vacating New Deal programs appeared that same year in *Norman v. Baltimore & O. Ry. Co.*,[274] which, by a 5-4 vote, upheld the Emergency Banking Act of 1933, which voided so-called "gold clauses" in contracts and allowed the payment of debts in legal tender. The conservative trend picked up again in 1935, with *Railroad Retirement Bd. v. Alton R.R. Co.*,[275] in which Roberts joined the four horsemen in condemning the Railroad Retirement Act of 1934 that provided for railroad worker pensions.[276]

But the first full-scale disaster for Roosevelt's economic relief and recovery aspirations hit on the last day of the Court's October 1934 Term, May 27, 1935. On that day, which Jackson named "Black Monday," the Bench declared three especially important New Deal measures unconstitutional.[277] In *Louisville Bank v. Radford*,[278] the Court nullified the Frazier-Lemke Act that provided much needed relief for farm mortgagors. In *Humphrey's Executor v. United States*,[279] the majority held that Roosevelt was without power to remove a reactionary Federal Trade Commission member from official ser-

---

273. 293 U.S. 389 (1935).
274. 294 U.S. 240 (1935).
275. 295 U.S. 330 (1935).
276. Hughes, Brandeis, Stone, and Cardozo dissented.
277. This trilogy may profitably be compared with the conservative 1819 trilogy, the liberal 1837 trilogy, and the conservative 1895 trilogy discussed earlier.
278. 295 U.S. 555 (1935).
279. 295 U.S. 602 (1935).

vice. Finally, in the most significant decision of the three, *Schechter Poultry Corp. v. United States*,[280] the Court threw out the National Industrial Recovery Act, the heart of the New Deal's program for dealing with industrial unemployment and lack of production. Further, following the Supreme Court's lead, the lower courts proceeded to attempt to bring Congress and the nation's executive officers to a halt. In 1935 and 1936 alone, "[S]ixteen hundred injunctions restraining officers of the Federal Government from carrying out acts of Congress were granted by Federal Judges."[281]

The debacle continued throughout the October 1935 Term.[282] On January 6, 1936, the Court handed down *United States v. Butler*[283] holding the Agricultural Adjustment Act unconstitutional. This decision, in which both Hughes and Roberts closed ranks with the four horsemen, has been described by Jackson as "a crushing disappointment to the Administration."[284] The A.A.A., which provided desperately needed price supports and subsidies for farmers, had been one of the proudest achievements of the New Deal and one of the major causes of the rural recovery that took root in America from 1933 to 1935. Yet, the attorney for the A.A.A.'s opponents, George Wharton Pepper, speaking in tones reminiscent of Choate in the 1895 income tax case, charged that approval of the measure would be equivalent to the end of freedom:

> *Indeed, may it please your Honors, I believe I am standing here today to plead the cause of the America I have loved; and I pray Almighty God that not in my time may 'the land of the regimented' be accepted as a worthy substitute for 'the land of the free.'*[285]

The Court's opinion declaring the A.A.A. unconstitutional was based on the concept that the nation's agriculture was a

---

280. 295 U.S. 495 (1935).
281. Jackson, *The Struggle for Judiciary Supremacy*, at 115.
282. *Id.* at 124-75.
283. 297 U.S. 1 (1936).
284. Jackson, *The Struggle for Judiciary Supremacy*, at 125.
285. 297 U.S. at 44.

local problem over which the federal government had no power whatever. In so holding, the Court temporarily rendered the Roosevelt Administration impotent to deal with the crucial problem of food production.

The next disaster for the New Deal was *Jones v. SEC*.[286] The issue presented in this case was whether an individual charged with stock fraud under the Securities Act could escape investigation, exposure, and punishment simply by withdrawing the registration statement containing the false representations. In a 6-3 decision, the Court struck an almost disabling blow at the Securities Exchange Commission by holding that withdrawal of the statement prevented the SEC from taking any further action. Moreover, the opinion of Justice Sutherland viciously attacked the behavior of the SEC.

The *Jones* case was followed by *Carter v. Carter Coal Co.*,[287] which held the Bituminous Coal Conservation Act unconstitutional. The statute in question was particularly important for the New Deal, since it dealt with problems in the coal mining industry that had in turn led to severe disorders and extreme misery on the part of the miners. Writing for the majority, Justice Sutherland declared the statute unconstitutional as an improper delegation of law-making power from Congress to the White House.

After then declaring the Municipal Bankruptcy Law unconstitutional,[288] the Court finished off its Term by striking down the New York Minimum Wage Law for Women in *Morehead v. New York ex rel. Tipaldo*.[289] Using, in by now almost classic style, the "freedom of contract" concept as a buttress against wage and hour legislation, Justice Butler, speaking for the five-vote majority, followed this conservative line:

> *In making contracts of employment, generally speaking, the parties have equal right to obtain from each other the best terms they can by private bargaining. Legislative abridgement of that freedom can only be justified by the existence of exceptional cir-*

---

286. 298 U.S. 1 (1936).
287. 298 U.S. 238 (1936).
288. Ashton v. Cameron County Dist., 298 U.S. 513 (1936).
289. 298 U.S. 587 (1936).

cumstances. Freedom of contract is the general rule and restraint the exception. [290]

As Jackson has stated in his account of the case:

This, of course, meant that the weak must bear the consequence of their weakness, and the strong may drive the best bargain that their strength and labor's necessities make possible. Labor relations were to be governed by the law of the jungle, and the state might not protect even women and children from exploitation. [291]

In his dissenting opinion, Justice Stone made much the same statement. He wrote:

There is grim irony in speaking of the freedom of contract of those who, because of their economic necessities, give their services for less than is needful to keep body and soul together. But if this is freedom of contract no one has ever denied that it is freedom which may be restrained, notwithstanding the Fourteenth Amendment, by a statute passed in the public interest. [292]

In short, during the mid-1930's, the Court carried out a major systematic attack on the New Deal, nullifying many of the leading legislative and executive efforts at economic reform. With the four horsemen in the van and Roberts on board, the forces of laissez faire conservatism swept to victory in case after case. Most of the cases were decided by narrow 5-4 or 6-4 majorities, but even the liberals deserted Roosevelt's standard of repudiating the National Industrial Recovery Act and signalling the executive and legislative branches that the collectivist program of the so-called First New Deal was unacceptable to the Court. A constitutional impasse was at hand.

The following table shows how the Justices tend to split during this period when the decisions were not unanimous:

---

290. *Id.* at 610-11.
291. Jackson, *The Struggle for Judiciary Supremacy,* at 172.
292. 298 U.S. at 632.

TABLE P

Alignment of Justices - Mid-1930's

Liberal	Moderate	Conservative
Brandeis	Hughes	McReynolds
Cardozo		Butler
Stone		Van Devanter
		Sutherland
		Roberts

In its attempt to destroy the New Deal, the Supreme Court majority relied heavily on three major conceptual weapons: (1) economic substantive due process, (2) unlawful encroachment on matters reserved for the states, and (3) unlawful delegation of legislative power. The notion of substantive due process was used to destroy the Frazier-Lemke Act (farm mortgage relief) in *Radford* and the Minimum Wage Law for Women in *Tipaldo*. Unlawful encroachment on areas reserved for the states was the basis for the overthrow of the A.A.A., the Bituminous Coal Conservation Act, the Municipal Bankruptcy Act, and the National Industrial Recovery Act in the *Butler, Carter, Ashton,* and *Schechter* cases. Unlawful delegation of legislative power provided a basis for the nullification of the N.I.R.A. and the "hot oil" statute in the *Schechter* and *Ryan* cases.

As Jackson summarized the situation:

> *Two kinds of power seem always in competition in our democracy: there is political power, which is the power of the voters, and there is the economic power of property, which is the power of its owners. Conflicts between the two bring much grist to the judicial mill. The basic grievance of the New Deal was that the Court has seemed unduly to favor private economic power and always to find ways of circumventing the efforts of popular government to control or regulate it.*
>
> *Thus, as we shall see, the Court conducted a dual campaign against the powers which the Congress thought had been granted to it by the Constitution. On the one hand, it narrowed the scope of the great clauses of the Constitution granting powers to Con-*

gress. It seriously contracted the interstate commerce power and it read startling exemptions into the taxing power. Simultaneously, it expanded the scope of clauses which limited the power of Congress, such as the 'due process clause' and the clauses withholding power from the federation. At the same time it used the 'due process' concept to cut down the effective power of the states. Divisions of opinion on constitutional interpretation ceased to be along the classic lines of a liberal as against a strict construction. The same justices used both in the interests of private economic power: they were strict and niggardly in the construing powers of government and liberal to the point of extravagance in construing limitations - even inventing such limitations as 'freedom of contract' where none existed in the Constitution.

It was this manifestation of judicial supremacy which threatened legislative and Executive paralysis and provoked the revolt against the Court's prevailing doctrine.[293]

---

293. Jackson, *The Struggle for Judiciary Supremacy*, at xii-xiii.

Part Five

The Second Liberal Era (1937-1969)

Chapter Eleven

The Constitutional Revolution of 1937[294]

> *It was not recognized at the time, but the Tipaldo case marked the end of the Court that Marshall had created. When the Justices left for their summer vacation in June of 1936 they almost certainly did not anticipate that never again (at least until 1965, the time of the present writing) would the Court employ the Constitution to interfere in any substantial extent with government of economic affairs. The era of judicial nullification of social welfare laws had come to an end.*[295]

The year 1937 marks, by all odds, the single most decisive turning point in the history of American constitutional law. The judicial events of that year fully merit the label "revolutionary," since they involved renunciation by the Court of the very activity that had been its most important and characteristic function for nearly fifty years, namely the exercise of a constitutional veto over economic legislation.

The stage for the constitutional revolution of 1937 was set by the national election of 1936. The people of the nation then, by a popular margin of nearly 8,000,000 votes and an electoral college margin of 523 to 8, ratified the New Deal and returned Franklin Delano Roosevelt to office with a mandate for massive government intervention designed to end the hard times and get the nation on its economic feet again. Yet, as Roosevelt returned to his task, he found himself faced with a Court that had persistently denied the nation's authority to undertake the economic experiment it wanted. A constitutional impasse had developed.

---

294. *See* Jackson, *The Struggle for Judicial Supremacy*, at 176-285.
295. Pfeffer, *This Honorable Court*, at 310.

On February 5, 1937, Roosevelt launched an attack on the Court by proposing legislation to increase the size of the Court from nine Justices to a possible fifteen and thus provide enough additional pro-New Deal votes to overthrow the control of the old guard on the Court.[296] In other words, Roosevelt threatened to "pack" the Court. All eyes then turned to the Bench to see what the reaction would be.

The Court watchers did not have long to wait. On March 29, 1937, in one of the most astounding turnabouts in American legal history, the Court upheld the State of Washington's minimum wage act for women and children, a statute "which was substantially identical to the New York Act declared unconstitutional [in*Tipaldo*] only the year before."[297] The decision, which as much as any other mentioned in this text merits the title of landmark case, was *West Coast Hotel Co. v. Parrish*.[298]

Elsie Parrish was a "chambermaid" at the West Coast Hotel. The hotel paid Ms. Parrish wages that did not satisfy Washington's "Minimum Wages for Women" statute. She sued for the difference. The hotel argued that the statute violated substantive due process, citing *Adkins v. Children's Hospital* (1923)[299] and *Tipaldo* (1936).[300] No doubt, under prior case law, the hotel was correct. *Adkins*, which had used substantive due process to invalidate the District of Columbia Minimum Wage Law, also involved a woman employed in a hotel. Moreover, *Tipaldo* had reaffirmed *Adkins* only the prior Term. Predictably, a lower court had already dismissed the case once.

The Supreme Court, by a narrow 5-4 margin, shocked the legal community by upholding the Washington minimum wage law. "[I]f such laws," the majority stated, "have a reasonable relation to a proper legislative purpose, and are neither arbitrary nor discriminatory, the requirements of due

---

296. In his initial message to Congress, Roosevelt tried to skirt the real issue by claiming that the purpose of adding new Justices was merely to provide more energy for the burdened Court. On March 9, 1937, however, Roosevelt admitted to the nation that the real purpose was to change the law.

297. Jackson, *The Struggle for Judiciary Supremacy*, at 191.

298. 300 U.S. 379 (1937).

299. 261 U.S. 525 (1923); see p. 119 *supra*.

300. 298 U.S. 587 (1936); see pp. 128-29 *supra*.

process are satisfied...."[301] The principle was not new. It was the familiar rational basis test that the pre-1937 Court had used with such vengeance. The revolutionary dimension inherent in the ruling was the explicit adoption by the Court of a deferential attitude in applying the test. A strong presumption of constitutionality, the Court held, applies to statutes regulating employment contracts. As the majority opinion put it:

> In dealing with the relation of employer and employed, the legislature had necessarily a wide field of discretion.... [A statute regulating such a relationship] may not be annulled unless palpably in excess of legislative power.... [E]very possible presumption is in favor of its validity....[302]

This, of course, was directly contrary to Adkins, which held, "Freedom of contract is...the general rule and restraint the exception."[303] And that was precisely the revolutionary advance. Applying their new deferential rational basis test, five Justices found Washington's minimum wage law reasonable. The majority ended its opinion by explicitly overruling Adkins. The four horsemen, to no one's surprise, dissented.

West Coast Hotel Co. v. Parrish merits attention not only because it was the first major decision in the constitutional revolution of 1937 but even more because the ruling destroyed the centerpiece of conservative constitutional activism, economic substantive due process. This principle had been the pre-1937 Court's most powerful weapon in the battle against state economic reform legislation. By converting the old presumption of unconstitutionality of socio-economic statutes into a strong, opposite presumption of constitutionality, Parrish brought to a close the era of conservative due process activism that had persisted, with only a few lapses, since 1890.

Any feeling that Parrish might be only a momentary respite for the New Deal was laid to rest by subsequent cases. A mere two weeks later, on April 12, 1937, the Court announced the

---

301. 300 U.S. at 398.
302. Id. at 398, 400.
303. 261 U.S. 525, 546 (1923).

important decision in *National Labor Relations Bd. v. Jones & Laughlin Steel Corp.*,[304] which dramatically expanded the federal power to regulate commerce, upheld the National Labor Relations Act (Wagner Act), and provided "the most far-reaching victory ever won on behalf of labor in the Supreme Court."[305] The Court then proceeded before the end of the Term to sustain both state and federal unemployment compensation laws and the old age benefit provisions of the federal Social Security Act.[306] In each of these cases, the vote was 5-4, with Brandeis, Stone, Cardozo, Hughes, and Roberts *versus* Sutherland, Butler, Van Devanter, and McReynolds.

The basic constitutional policy that captured the Court in 1937 has remained dominant to the present day. According to this doctrine, it is not proper for the judiciary to nullify duly enacted state or federal socio-economic statutes simply because the Justices believe they unreasonably interfere with economic liberty or with matters of allegedly local concern. Henceforward, rights of property were demoted from the preferred - almost sacred - position they had held since the days of empiricist philosopher John Locke and placed alongside the other interests which are subject to adjustment and compromise through the legislative process.

How could this fundamental change occur without a single change in Court personnel? The answer is surprisingly simple, albeit somewhat disillusioning for those who believe that the law should be based on stable principles of reason: one Justice changed his mind.

Immediately prior to 1937, three Supreme Court Justices had led the opposition to the dominant doctrine of laissez faire, Brandeis, Stone, and Cardozo. During the October 1935 Term, the unpredictable Chief Justice Hughes had vacillated between the Court's liberal and conservative wings, often leaving only the narrowest 5-4 margin favoring the latter's view. All that was needed to create the revolution was for one Justice to change sides. That one Justice turned out to be Owen Roberts, who affiliated with the liberals in *West Coast Hotel Co. v. Par-*

---

304. 301 U.S. 1 (1937).

305. Jackson, *The Struggle for Judiciary Supremacy,* at 214.

306. Carmichael v. Southern Coal Co., 301 U.S. 495 (1937) (state unemployment insurance); Steward Machine Co. v. Davis, 301 U.S. 548 (1937) (federal unemployment compensation); Helvering v. Davis, 301 U.S. 619 (1937) (old-age benefits).

rish and subsequent cases, giving them the majority they had so long been lacking.

Shortly thereafter, events occurred insuring that the constitutional revolution of 1937 would be a durable one. Perhaps sensing their cause was doomed, the old guard began retiring. The first to go was Justice Van Devanter, who departed at the end of the Term. Van Devanter had served as a reliable member of the four horseman, and his loss left a gaping hole in their ranks. Roosevelt then stunned conservatives in general by appointing to the empty seat the radical New Deal Senator and Alabama "people's lawyer," Hugo Lafayette Black (1937-71), a man who was far to the left of even Justice Brandeis.[307] During early 1938, Justice Sutherland followed Van Devanter into retirement and was replaced by another New Dealer, Stanley F. Reed (1938-57).[308] These and subsequent Roosevelt appointments eradicated all possibilities of a short term counterrevolution.

The fabric of the new majority's economic jurisprudence was woven out of several key conceptual strands. The doctrine of economic substantive due process and the related doctrine of liberty of contract were almost completely discarded.[309] The commerce clause was invested once again with the broad sweep that Chief Justice Marshall had established more than a century earlier.[310] Other federal powers were given a similarly

---

307. For a particularly intimate account of Justice Black's life and thought, *see* Hugo Black, Jr., *My Father*, (New York: Random House, 1975). In his book, Hugo Black, Jr. describes his father as a timeless economic radical who conceived of government as a process designed to support the common people in their endless struggle to control the tendency of wealth to concentrate and create exploitative social systems. *Id.* at 140 *et seq.* Justice Black believed, "[T]he combined power of organized wealth and its organized propaganda never ceases to fight every intelligent effort to save us from the terrible abuses incident to the exploitation of the many by the powerful few." *Id.* at 147.

Black distrusted wealth, distrusted businessmen, opposed depreciation deductions and the inheritance of wealth, and rejected the traditional conservative trickle down theory: "We don't have to bribe the rich to let them get richer." *Id.* at 146. "When Daddy arrived (on the Supreme Court)...he determined to do all he could to make the Supreme Court a haven for the helpless, weak...." *Id.* at 182. Black was the most liberal member of the Court when he was seated, and he remained a member of the Court's liberal wing until the last few years of his long tenure.

308. Reed was far more liberal than Sutherland, whom he replaced, but he was "no left winger." Pfeffer, *This Honorable Court*, at 330.

309. *E.g.*, State Tax Comm'n. v. Aldrich, 316 U.S. 174 (1942); Olsen v. Nebraska, 313 U.S. 236 (1941); Curry v. McCanless, 307 U.S. 357 (1939); Driscoll v. Edison Light & Power Co., 307 U.S. 104 (1939); West Coast Hotel Co., v. Parrish, 300 U.S. 379 (1937).

310. *E.g.*, American Power & Light Co. v. SEC, 329 U.S. 90 (1946); Wickard v. Filburn, 317 U.S. 111 (1942); Mulford v. Smith, 307 U.S. 38 (1939); NLRB v. Jones & Laughlin Steel Corp. 301 U.S. 1 (1937).

broad interpretation, including the taxing and spending powers, the war power, and the foreign relations power.[311] The notion that the tenth amendment restricts the federal government by reserving large areas of legislative action exclusively for the states was rejected.[312] The doctrine of unconstitutional delegation of legislative power was similarly dropped.[313]

The Court's deferential attitude toward economic legislation was applied not only to the federal government but to the states as well. The elimination of the substantive due process/liberty of contract doctrine freed the states from far-reaching restraints[314] as did the softening of dormant commerce clause restrictions.[315] In short, the Roosevelt Court withdrew from the role of constitutional censor of socio-economic legislation, adopting instead the posture of judicial restraint characteristic of Holmesian liberalism.

The turnabout marked a milestone and major victory for the poor in their long struggle for greater justice at the bar of the Supreme Court. It cleared the way for social legislation designed to insure, to an ever greater degree, that all persons are able to obtain at least the basic economic prerequisites to a decent life. No longer would the advocates of economic reform need to fear that their hard-won legislative victories would be nullified by a small cadre of partisan Supreme Court Justices.

Although this constitutional revolution, for all practical purposes, eliminated the old economic issues from consideration, it did not eliminate the rich/poor controversy from the Supreme Court's calendar. However, the specific issues changed. Henceforth, the Court's greatest impact in the economic arena derived from its authority to interpret and enforce legislation. Since it is often impossible to draft completely unambiguous statutes, the Supreme Court retains substantial power to control the impact of socio-economic legislation

---

311. *E.g.*, Helvering v. Davis, 301 U.S. 619 (1937) (taxing and spending power); Steward Machine Co. v. Davis, 301 U.S. 548 (1937) (taxing and spending power).

312. *E.g.*, United States v. Darby Lumber Co., 312 U.S. 100 (1941).

313. *E.g.*, Yakus v. United States, 321 U.S. 414 (1944); H.P. Hood & Sons v. United States, 307 U.S. 588 (1939).

314. *See* cases cited *supra* note 309.

315. *E.g.*, Nelson v. Sears, Roebuck & Co., 312 U.S. 359 (1941); McGoldrick v. Berwind-White Coal Co., 309 U.S. 33 (1940); South Carolina Highway Dept. v. Barnwell Bros., 303 U.S. 177 (1938).

through the alchemy of judicial interpretation. Moreover, important new issues having indirect but significant impacts on the rich/poor struggle emerged in the post-1937 period, issues concerning race relations, voting rights, criminal procedure, and the like. These issues were destined to provide opportunities for new and less conspicuous forms of economic liberalism and conservatism to appear.

Chapter Twelve

The Roosevelt Court (1937-1946)[316]

Roosevelt's initial triumph in acquiring for his New Deal programs the judicial approval he had sought for so long was achieved without his having to make a single change in Court personnel. He was soon able, however, to reinforce his accomplishment by engineering what was perhaps the most dramatic political and philosophical shift among the nine Justices ever to occur in a relatively short period of American history.

During the years between 1937 and 1948, Roosevelt made eight appointments to the Court,[317] beginning with Hugo Black, perhaps the most liberal figure to serve as a Justice up until that time, and Stanley Reed, the Solicitor General who had represented the government in many court challenges to New Deal programs.

In the years after the two were seated, openings on the Court continued to come thick and fast. In 1938, Cardozo died. He was succeeded by Felix Frankfurter (1939-62), a political liberal, an important Roosevelt advisor, and a draftsman of much New Deal legislation.[318] That same year, Brandeis retired. Roosevelt named to his seat the equally liberal William O. Douglas (1939-75), another New Deal brain truster, who had

---

316. A principal source of the material presented in this chapter is C. Herman Pritchett, *The Roosevelt Court* (Chicago: Quadrangle Books, 1948).

317. Other than Roosevelt, only George Washington made this many appointments.

318. Frankfurter was one of the most politically liberal men appointed by Roosevelt. However, because of a deeply rooted Holmesian belief in judicial restraint, Frankfurter became a conservative Justice. Thus, the Cardozo-Frankfurter succession comprised a move to the right, the only one among the Roosevelt personnel changes.

served previously on the SEC.[319] In 1939, a third member of the conservative old guard, Justice Butler, died. To fill the vacancy, Roosevelt selected still another reformer, the liberal former governor of Michigan, Frank Murphy (1939-49).[320] Roosevelt appointees were now a majority on the Court.

In 1941, moderate Chief Justice Charles Evans Hughes retired. His position was filled by the promotion of Harlan F. Stone, who had been affiliated with the Court's liberal wing ever since his appointment as Associate Justice in 1925. The seat vacated by the promotion was then given to former Solicitor General Robert H. Jackson (1941-54).[321] Finally, the last of the four horsemen, McReynolds, retired. James F. Byrnes (1941-42), one of Roosevelt's closest political confidantes, was chosen to replace him. Byrnes elected to serve on the Court for only one year, after which he was followed by Wiley Rutledge (1943-49), another consistent liberal.[322]

The following table illustrates the remarkable shift in judicial viewpoints on purely economic matters brought about by Roosevelt midway through his tenure:

---

319. Douglas was a "champion of the weak against the strong." Black, *My Father*, at 242. As Black put it, "He'll always vote for a labor union, because he thinks government has got to sponsor power to countervail against privilege." *Id.* A first hand account of Douglas' deep identification with the poor can be found in his *Go East, Young Man* (New York: Dell Publishing Co., 1974), in which he states he was "aligned...emotionally with the miserable people who make up the chaff of society." *Id.* at 62. This theme comes through at many points in Douglas' writings. To cite only one more example,"My heart was with the impoverished, restless underdogs who were the IWW's." *Id.* at 78. Douglas was the Court's most liberal Justice for more than twenty years at the end of his tenure.

320. *See* 4 Friedman & Israel, *The Justices of the United States*, at 2493-2506. Murphy soon became a member of the liberal activist wing along with Black and Douglas. In fact, he was arguably "the most brilliant liberal on the Court." He had been an ardent New Dealer and on the bench he aligned himself with Black and Douglas as a steadfast champion of civil liberties." *This Honorable Court*, at 342.

321. Once on the Court, Jackson, like Frankfurter and Reed, became relatively conservative. The following quotes concerning labor and judicial restraint illustrate Jackson's moderate, restrained position. "[M]y feeling [was] that labor was no more to be trusted than capital to conform its policies to good social practices...." Quoted in 4 Friedman & Israel, *The Justices of the United States*, at 2551. "In general I agreed with Chief Justice Stone that activism was no more appropriate on the part of the judiciary in favor of reforms than it was in knocking them down." Quoted in *id.* at 2565.

322. Rutledge was an "outspoken defender of the 'underdog.' " 4 Friedman & Israel, *The Justices of the United States*, at 2595. He was a strong economic liberal, favorable toward the New Deal, favorable toward powerful administrative agencies, favorable toward labor. "On the bench Rutledge aligned himself with Black, Douglas and Murphy as a staunch champion...of the 1937 revolution." Pfeffer, *This Honorable Court*, at 346.

TABLE Q

Alignment of Justices Serving in 1943

Liberal	Moderate	Conservative
Murphy	Roberts[323]	
Rutledge		
Black		
Douglas		
Reed		
Frankfurter		
Jackson		
Stone		

Clearly, the Court's second conservative era was finished. By 1943 the assembly serving on the Court was the most liberal in the Court's history.[324] The Bench's second liberal era was well underway.

The first task awaiting the Roosevelt majority was simply to confirm the rule established in 1937 of judicial restraint in economic matters. This job was carried out in a consistent and explicit manner, leaving no doubt that the Court had withdrawn from its role of censor over economic legislation.

In 1939, for example, the Court upheld the Agricultural Adjustment Act of 1938, which, among other things, set production quotas for tobacco producers.[325] Such regulations of local production could not have survived the Court's scrutiny during the early 1930's. In that same year, the Court sustained the power of Congress to delegate to the Department of Agriculture broad authority to regulate prices of goods moving in interstate commerce.[326] Similarly, "the Court sustained the constitutionality of a municipal bankruptcy law in all essentials the same as one it had held unconstitutional two years before."[327] These and other similar cases attest to the validity

323. Roberts is counted as a moderate here because of his change of position in early 1937. He was previously listed as a conservative. *See* p. 130 *supra.*

324. The Taney Court after 1837 may have been more liberal on occasion. No other Court is even in contention.

325. Mulford v. Smith, 307 U.S. 38 (1939).

326. United States v. Rock Royal Co-op, 307 U.S. 533 (1939).

327. United States v. Bekins, 304 U.S. 27 (1938). The quotation is from Jackson, *The Struggle for Judicial Supremacy,* at 240.

of Pfeffer's assertion that after 1937, "the era of judicial nullification of social welfare laws had come to an end."[328]

A case which epitomizes the constitutional posture of the Roosevelt Court in the economic arena is *United States v. F.W. Darby Lumber Co.* (1941),[329] the landmark case that upheld the federal Fair Labor Standards Act of 1938. The statute was the last major New Deal economic reform law enacted by Congress. It imposed sweeping wage and hour restraints on businesses affecting commerce. Prior to 1937, this statute would have been held to violate substantive due process and the tenth amendment and to exceed Congress' power under the commerce clause. Stone's majority opinion in *Darby* rejected each of these theories in forceful terms.

Substantive due process was brushed aside in the following curt passage: "Since our decision in West Coast Hotel v. Parrish....it is no longer open to question that the fixing of a minimum wage is within the legislative power.... Nor is it any longer open to question that it is within the legislative power to fix maximum hours."[330] The pre-1937 notion of dual federalism derived from the tenth amendment was rejected in even stronger terms: "Our conclusion is unaffected by the Tenth Amendment.... The amendment states but a truism.... [F]or many years (i.e., since 1937) the amendment has been construed as not depriving the national government of authority to resort to all means for the exercise of a granted power which are appropriate and plainly adapted to the permitted end."[331] Finally, the Court adopted an extremely broad reading of "the plenary power conferred on Congress by the Commerce Clause."[332] Holding that Congress has broad power to regulate even local activities which affect interstate commerce, the Court stated: "The power of Congress over interstate commerce is complete in itself, may be exercised to its utmost extent, and acknowledges no limitations other than are prescribed in the Constitution."[333]

---

328. Pfeffer, *This Honorable Court*, at 310.
329. 312 U.S. 100 (1941).
330. *Id.* at 125.
331. *Id.* at 123-24.
332. *Id.* at 115.
333. *Id.* at 114; *cf.* Wickard v. Filburn, 317 U.S. 311 (1942).

The *Darby* opinion was, then, a veritable graveyard for the leading economic ideas of the pre-1937 Court. Moreover, the ruling indicated that fair labor standards, including minimum wage and maximum hour provisions, had reached a milestone in their long and circuitous journey through the courts and had apparently arrived at a safe constitutional haven.

The Roosevelt Court's enthusiasm for the administration's brand of economic thinking went far beyond the mere discarding of pre-1937 constitutional restraints on socio-economic legislation. There still remained the vastly important task of construing and enforcing the sweeping legislation characteristic of the age of big government. Here the majority took the position that these measures were to be broadly construed. Again and again, the prevailing Justices insisted upon vigorous enforcement of economic reform statutes, giving especially strong support to legislative and executive programs of business and trade regulation.[334]

The Justices' predominant economic liberalism was perhaps most evident in cases involving labor unions.[335] Roughly a decade and a half earlier, Chief Justice Taft had described labor unions as a group that the Court had to "hit every little while" to keep them in line. The Roosevelt Court, in contrast, took such an opposite tack as to lead the greatest constitutional scholar of the period, Edward S. Corwin, to write: "Constitutional law has always had a central interest to guard. Today it appears to be that of organized labor."[336]

Among the pro-labor cases leading to Corwin's conclusion were *Apex Hosiery Co. v. Leader* (1940),[337] which overturned a long string of precedents and held union activities to be exempt from the "restraint of trade" prohibitions of the Sherman Act; and *Thornhill v. Alabama* (1940),[338] which found peaceful

---

334. *E.g.,* Gemsco, Inc. v. Walling, 324 U.S. 244 (1945) (Administrator, FLSA); FPC v. Hope Natural Gas Co., 320 U.S. 591 (1944) (FPC); NBC v. United States, 319 U.S. 190 (1943) (FCC); FPC v. Natural Gas Pipeline Co., 315 U.S. 575 (1942) (FPC); Gray v. Powell, 314 U.S. 402 (1941) (Bituminous Coal Division); United States v. Morgan, 313 U.S. 409 (1941) (USDA). See Pritchett, *The Roosevelt Court,* at 167-197, which discusses "[t]he generally favorable attitude of the Roosevelt Court toward administrative legislation."

335. Another major area was civil rights. After 1937, the attention of the judicial "activists" turned increasingly toward protection of civil rights.

336. Edward S. Corwin, *The Constitution and What It Means Today* (New York: Atheneum, 1965), at viii.

337. 310 U.S. 469 (1940).

338. 310 U.S. 88 (1940).

picketing to be a form of speech subject to the special protection of the first amendment. Now, the days when the wealthy classes could look to the Supreme Court as the final bastion of defense against the efforts of the masses to redistribute power and property were gone - at least for the time being.

But, for all the radical changes they wrought in judicial thinking as regards the roles and responsibilities of government's various branches, it would be mistaken to conclude that the New Deal Justices were continually of one mind on all issues. True, the most moderate of Roosevelt's appointees were far more liberal than the four horsemen who preceded them and, true, during that 1937-39 period, the President's first five appointees, Black, Reed, Frankfurter, Douglas, and Murphy tended overwhelmingly to vote as a bloc. Nevertheless, after 1940, the Justices began slowly to split into two distinct groups, one reflecting a spirit of judicial activism, the other tempered by a belief in restraint. Black and Douglas were charter members of the activist faction. Murphy soon joined them, and Rutledge came aboard in 1943. Frankfurter and Reed were the charter members of the "moderation through restraint" opposition. They were soon joined by Jackson. Meanwhile, Roberts drifted again in the direction of increased conservatism. As a result of these developments, the Court line-up from 1943 to 1945 was as follows:

TABLE R

Alignment of Justices - 1943 to 1945

Liberal	Moderate	Conservative
Murphy	Reed	Roberts
Rutledge	Jackson	
Douglas	Frankfurter	
Black	Stone	

So as World War II was drawing to a close, and as Roosevelt's death approached, the question of how far the Justices should go in pursuing liberal goals was becoming the central issue on the Court.

Chapter Thirteen

The Vinson Court (1946-1953)[339]

During the late 1940's, the United States entered a period of political and economic conservatism. After World War II, instead of peace came "Cold War." The communist nations, which had been allied with America in the struggle against Nazi Germany, now appeared to many as a monolithic force bent on subjugating the entire world. The United States, in general, underwent a kind of collective psychosis in which subversives were suspected of hiding behind every bush and under every table. The hysteria took hold in the late 1940's and climaxed in the early 1950's when Senator Joseph McCarthy dominated the nation as few individuals have ever done and held power to destroy lives simply by accusing persons of being communists or merely communist sympathizers.

During these years which saw even President Eisenhower portrayed as a communist dupe, advocacy of any kind of government sponsored economic reform became dangerous indeed. The prevailing conservative mood spilled over into the political arena in a variety of ways. In the 1946 off-year elections, the Republicans took control of both houses of Congress and soon enacted legislation "that expressed the general conservative reaction against the New Deal era."[340] Anti-labor sentiment produced the Taft-Hartley Act of 1947, which banned the closed shop and imposed liability on unions for breaches of

---

339. For more detailed discussions of the Vinson era, *see* C. Herman Pritchett, *Civil Liberties and the Vinson Court* (Chicago: University of Chicago Press, 1954); Galloway, *The Vinson Court: Polarization (1946-1949) and Conservative Dominance (1949-1953)*, 22 Santa Clara L. Rev. 375 (1982).

340. 2 Hofstadter, Miller & Aaron, *The American Republic*, at 642.

collective bargaining agreements. Truman's "Fair Deal" economic reform package, an aggregate of agricultural, labor, and civil rights measures, died in Congress. As the years passed, advocacy of continued economic reform carried with it the risk of being blacklisted, which in turn often meant a loss of employment and community status.

The reactionary drift of the McCarthy Era was so powerful that no Court could have deflected it from its course. Nevertheless, a vigilant set of Justices might have curbed at least some of its excesses. The Court majority of the McCarthy Era, however, was of a significantly different stripe from its immediate predecessor. Eventually bolstered by four surprisingly conservative Truman appointees, the Court's more conservative wing took control and backed away from the liberal activism that had been such a strong characteristic of the Roosevelt Court.

By the late 1940's, the strength of the Court's liberal wing was waning. As will be recalled, the Roosevelt Court had become increasingly divided on the subject of the proper role of the federal judiciary. At mid-decade, a five-vote coalition of moderate voices was generally able to prevent the emergence of any revolutionary judicial liberal activism.

Subsequent appointments to the Bench by President Harry S. Truman then substantially enhanced the power of the Court's "less liberal" wing. In 1945, Roberts retired. Truman, in a fit of bi-partisanship, secured the open position for Harold H. Burton (1945-58), a Republican Senator who promptly affiliated with the Court's new "conservative" wing. In 1946, Chief Justice Harlan F. Stone, by now an economic moderate, died. Truman selected the more conservative Fred Vinson (1946-53) to replace him. Vinson, a former New Deal Congressman and circuit court judge, had been one of Truman's closest advisors in the first months of his presidency, and he continued to consult with Truman on policy matters after becoming Chief Justice. Vinson soon became the dominant member of the so-called "Vinson bloc" and the most powerful Justice of the Court. Both Burton and Vinson were advocates of judicial restraint in the pre-1937 sense of the concept. That is, they were essentially Holmesian liberals, but they were definitely not activists. Their arrival made it far easier for the moderates to restrain any Supreme Court crusade for the social and economic underdog.

From 1946 to 1949, the Justices tended to divide along the lines shown in the following table:

TABLE S

Alignment of Justices - 1946-1949

Liberal	Moderate	Conservative[341]
Murphy		Jackson
Rutledge		Frankfurter
Douglas		Vinson
Black		Burton
		Reed

The seating of Burton and Vinson triggered an immediate shift to the right in the Court's voting patterns. In the October 1946 Term, for example, the number of dissents by the Bench's most liberal Justices, Rutledge and Murphy, leaped upward to a level double that of the previous Term.[342] The swing to the right was probably most pronounced in civil liberties cases, but it was detectable in economic cases as well.

The Vinson Court's growing economic conservatism, however, was not of the same vintage of that of the 1890's, 1920's, or 1930's. Foremost among the differences was that the role of censor of economic legislation was not reassumed. Indeed, the Holmesian principle of judicial restraint in such matters continued to exert an extraordinary influence on the Court's thinking.

Why, then, refer to the Vinson Court as increasingly conservative? The explanation is that the concepts of economic liberalism and conservatism had taken on new meanings after the constitutional revolution of 1937. Traditional economic conservatism - i.e., constitutional activism on behalf of the rich - lost virtually all of its support after 1937 and for the

341. After the disappearance of the pre-1937 conservatives, the Vinson and Frankfurter blocs occupied the Court's right wing and became identified as conservatives. This group will henceforth be called conservative, keeping in mind, however, that this is a post-1937 conservatism, not the activist brand that characterized the pre-1937 Court.

342. Murphy's dissent rate jumped from 9.2% to 23.0%. Rutledge's dissent rate rose from 14.9% to 28.9%. In contrast, Frankfurter's dissent rate went down slightly. *See* Galloway, *supra* note 339 at 377.

most part vanished from the United States' judicial landscape. Henceforth, the policy of activism on behalf of the poor and the disenfranchised, which was endorsed by Justices Douglas, Black, and others, came to characterize the liberal viewpoint. And the policy of judicial restraint became the hallmark of modern judicial conservatism. The Vinson Court was conservative in this new post-1937 sense.

The Vinson Court's swing toward economic conservatism can be traced back as far as *United States v. United Mine Workers* (1947),[343] which upheld an injunction against a UMW strike and the imposition of fines against the union's president, John L. Lewis, and his organization for breaches of that injunction. The case marked a major departure from the pro-labor stance that had been representative of the Roosevelt Court, particularly since even Black and Douglas deserted the liberal camp, leaving Murphy and Rutledge in isolated minority. The *UMW* ruling typified the Vinson Court's particular brand of economic conservatism through its use of legislative interpretation to achieve results consistent with the nation's prevailing anti-labor mood, rather than the use of constitutional barriers to nullify applicable labor statutes, as the pre-1937 Supreme Court was inclined to do.

Adamson v. California (1947)[344] provides a second classic illustration of the early Vinson Court's rejection of liberal activism. At issue in this conflict was whether the fifth amendment self-incrimination clause was binding on the states, but the broader, underlying issue was whether the entire Bill of Rights, with its many important protections for individual citizens, was applicable to the states. In a dissent that achieved landmark status for the ideas it introduced into judicial thinking, Justice Black, with concurrences by Douglas, Murphy, and Rutledge, pled eloquently for a constitutional revolution in criminal procedure by making the Bill of Rights applicable to the states. Nonetheless, the conservatives closed ranks and re-

---

343. 330 U.S. 258 (1947); *see* Pritchett, *The Roosevelt Court*, at 232-38. As early as 1948, *United Mine Workers* was recognized by Pritchett as a turning point and an indicator that the liberal Roosevelt Court had given way to a more conservative Vinson Court: "[A]lready the temper of the Court is changing, and a swing to the right is apparent in several fields.... At the moment my own guess is that the Roosevelt Court came to an end on that Thursday in March 1947, when the John L. Lewis decision was handed down." *Id.* at xiv.

344. 332 U.S. 46 (1947).

jected the plea. Once again, a new conservatism was reflected in the ruling. The Constitution was not invoked here to render a legislative measure void; rather, the majority declined to move in an activist manner to nullify government action. *Adamson* further typified the post-1937 judicial situation in that its economically conservative effects resulted indirectly from the Court's attitude toward civil liberties rather than from a majority favoritism for the rich.

In 1949, the Court's shift to the right became a rout. In the summer of that year, the liberal forces were decimated by the sudden deaths of Murphy and Rutledge. To succeed them, Truman selected two moderately conservative Justices, Tom C. Clark (1949-67), a former Texas lawyer and United States Attorney General, and Sherman Minton (1949-56), a former Indiana Senator and Seventh Circuit judge. Thus, the Court that was to preside during the McCarthy witchhunts had its liberal wing reduced to only two Justices, while its remaining seven members embraced a predominantly conservative outlook as regards the civil liberties issues that were suddenly of major national importance.

TABLE T

Alignment of Justices - 1949 to 1953

Liberal	Moderate	Conservative
Douglas		Vinson
Black		Burton
		Clark
		Minton
		Reed
		Jackson
		Frankfurter

For the next four years, the conservatives were to have their way. Using their clear numerical superiority effectively, they outright dominated the Court. Vinson, the Bench's most powerful member and leader of a five-vote bloc that included Burton, Clark, Minton, and Reed, dissented only infrequently. In contrast, the number of dissents registered by Douglas and Black leaped to modern record levels.

The leading case in the Court's continued move to the right was *Dennis v. United States* (1951),[345] which upheld the conviction of 11 leaders of the American Communist Party under the Smith Act. The statute prohibited (1) advocacy of the doctrine that the government should be overthrown by force and (2) membership in any organization advocating that doctrine. The trial attracted enormous national attention during 1949, and the convictions were upheld by the Supreme Court against challenges based on the first amendment. The majority opinion adopted a new constitutional test that allowed conviction without a clear and present danger of illegal action.

For the country at that time, the central significance of this decision was that it announced in unmistakable terms that the Vinson Court did not intend to interfere with the burgeoning harassment of both real subversives and economic reformers who were also the victims of the reactionary tide. Thus McCarthy was left with an essentially free hand. The effect of McCarthy's ensuing assaults against advocates of continued government programs of assistance to the poor cannot be measured. Nevertheless, it seems clear in retrospect that the threat of being labelled and attacked as a communist or communist sympathizer deterred all but the most hardy from pressing for any major economic changes.

---

345. 341 U.S. 494 (1951).

Chapter Fourteen

The Warren Court (1953-1969)[346]

Over the course of the Supreme Court's second liberal era, however, the rule of "conservatism through restraint" was destined to be only temporary. In much the same manner that the 1906-1920 "not quite progressive era" proved to be little more than a passing exception in a period of predominantly conservative activism on the Supreme Court, the Vinson approach to civil liberties and economics was soon superseded by the Warren Court's more liberal approach.

From 1953 to 1957, a renewed trend toward liberal activism appeared on the Court. This resurgence was made possible by President Dwight D. Eisenhower. In 1953, Chief Justice Vinson died. For his successor, Eisenhower chose the most liberal Chief Justice since Taney, Earl Warren (1953-69), the former governor of California.[347] After spending two Terms in the Court's ideological center, Warren moved into close alignment with Black and Douglas and remained there until his resignation in 1969. The liberal-activist wing was back up to three.

In 1954, Justice Jackson died. Since his replacement, John M. Harlan (1955-71), was also a conservative, no change was brought about in the Court's ideological alignment. Harlan, a Wall Street lawyer, moved directly to the Court's far right in his first Term and remained there throughout most of his tenure.

---

346. For useful general discussions of the Warren era, *see* Alexander M. Bickel, *Politics and the Warren Court* (New York: Da Capo Press, 1973); Archibald Cox, *The Warren Court* (Cambridge, Mass.: Harvard University Press, 1968); Philip B. Kurland, *Politics, the Constitution, and the Warren Court* (Chicago: The University of Chicago Press, 1969).

347. Warren's identification with the common people developed very early in his life, in part as a result of observations of employee mistreatment by the Southern Pacific Railroad. Earl Warren, *The Memoirs of Chief Justice Earl Warren* (New York: Doubleday & Company Inc., 1977), at 30-31. Warren's political hero was Hiram Johnson, leader of the California progressive movement, and Warren considered himself to be a progressive throughout his career.

Two years later, Sherman Minton retired, and Eisenhower appointed William J. Brennan (1956-), a former labor leader and liberal New Jersey state court judge, who brought a fourth vote to the Douglas, Black, and Warren wing.[348] The following table shows the line-up of Justices immediately after Brennan's arrival:

TABLE U
Alignment of Justices - 1956-1957

Liberal	Moderate	Conservative
Douglas	Clark[349]	Harlan
Black		Frankfurter
Warren		Burton
Brennan		Reed

Obviously, this Court was much more balanced than when a seven-two conservative majority held sway under Vinson. The liberals needed only one more vote to become a majority. During the mid-1950's, they were frequently able to pick up the ex-extra votes from Clark and Frankfurter and, in scattered cases, from other Justices.

There was, of course, no doubt from the start that the Warren Court would continue the pattern set in 1937 and decline to act as a constitutional censor of economic reform legislation.[350] As the majority was to state a few years later, "We have returned to the original proposition that courts do not substitute their social and economic beliefs for the judgment of legislative bodies, who are elected to pass laws."[351] Conservative activism of the pre-1937 vintage, in short, remained out of the question. The intriguing possibility, however, was that Warren and his supporters might adopt an activist, reforming brand of liberalism.

---

348. Brennan occupied a position nearer to the center than Douglas, Black, and Warren, but his basic alignment with the liberals was observable from his first Term.

349. Clark had been a member of the conservative wing during the Vinson era. When Warren joined the Court, Clark moved into a moderate position. In later years, Clark continued to oscillate between moderate and conservative positions.

350. *See*, e.g. Williamson v. Lee Optical Co., 348 U.S. 483 (1955).

351. Ferguson v. Skrupa, 372 U.S. 726, 730 (1963).

A shift away from conservative dominance became noticeable as early as the Court's October 1953 and 1954 Terms.[352] During the October 1955 and 1956 Terms, liberal activism was definitely on the return. For example, the landmark 1956 case *Griffin v. Illinois*[353] held that indigent criminal defendants are entitled to a free trial transcript for purposes of appeal. "There can be no equal justice," the Court stated, "where the kind of trial a man gets depends on the amount of money he has."[354] *Griffin* was the first in a long series of cases in which the Bench expanded the rights of indigent criminal defendants under the equal protection clause of the fourteenth amendment. The series is widely recognized as a prime indicator of the Warren Court's egalitarianism and liberal activism on behalf of the poor.[355]

The Warren Court of the mid-1950's also made a major effort to roll back the political repression characteristic of the times. The string of rulings relevant in this regard is too long to discuss in detail, but its leading cases deserve brief mention. In *Pennsylvania v. Nelson* (1956),[356] the Court held that the federal Smith Act pre-empted the field of anti-subversion legislation and nullified all state laws on the subject. In *Watkins v. United States* (1957),[357] the majority shook a stick at the notorious House Un-American Activities Committee, stating that Congress has no authority to investigate for purposes of punishment or to expose for purposes of mere exposure. That same day, in *Yates v. United States*,[358] the Bench drastically restricted the Smith Act by construing it to prohibit only incitement of "action" to overthrow the government, not advocacy of "abstract ideas." The pattern of *Nelson*, *Watkins*, and *Yates* was manifest in a series of additional decisions attempting to re-establish a basically open society in which economic and political alternatives could be discussed and advocated without fear of retaliation.[359]

---

352. See Galloway, *The Early Years of the Warren Court: Emergence of Judicial Liberalism (1953-1957)*, 18 Santa Clara L. Rev. 609, 612-16 (1978).

353. 351 U.S. 12 (1956).

354. *Id.*

355. *See, e.g.,* Cox, *The Warren Court*, at 7.

356. 350 U.S. 497 (1956).

357. 354 U.S. 178 (1957).

358. 354 U.S. 298 (1957).

359. These cases include Sweezy v. New Hampshire, 354 U.S. 234 (1957) (restricting state investigating committees); Jencks v. United States, 353 U.S. 657 (1957) (allowing ac-

The Court's efforts to turn back the repressive trends of the 1950's gave rise to an outburst of hostile public reaction.[360] The press was full of criticism. "Impeach Earl Warren" became a widely known slogan. Legislation was introduced to curb the power of the Court.[361] The assembled chief justices of the state supreme courts passed a resolution opposing liberal-activism on the Supreme Court. In response to the public furor, the Court quietly withdrew from its libertarian posture. The crossover members of the moderate and conservative ranks moved back to the right and increasingly deprived the liberals of their needed fifth vote. This relative quiescence was to prevail through 1961.[362]

Additional changes in Court personnel made toward the end of the 1950's helped sustain the Bench's withdrawal from liberal activism. In 1957, the by now conservative Reed retired. He was succeeded by Charles E. Whittaker (1957-62), a corporation lawyer from St. Louis. "Whittaker immediately aligned himself with the conservative justices on the Court."[363] He remained a member of that bloc throughout his brief tenure and, in fact, posted the Court's most conservative voting record during his final Term. Next, Burton retired in 1958. He was succeeded by Potter Stewart (1958-81), a Cincinnati Republican, Sixth Circuit judge, and moderate conservative.

The retreat that characterized the Warren Court's 1958 to 1961 middle period is reflected in a wide range of decisions. Two 1958 rulings upheld the dismissal of employees for refusal to answer questions regarding alleged communist activity.[364]

---

cess to FBI files to discover information provided by informers); Konigsberg v. State Bar, 353 U.S. 252 (1957) (restricting the denial of bar membership to alleged subversives); Schware v. Board of Educ., 353 U.S. 232 (1957) (same as *Konigsberg*); Slochower v. Board of Educ., 350 U.S. 551 (1956) (restricting the grounds for refusal of municipal employment).

360. This outburst was described by Professor Alpheus Mason as follows: "Dissenting Justices and constitutional lawyers are outspoken in protest; members of Congress are stunned though not silenced. Not since 1937 when F.D.R. declared war on the Nine Old Men, has judicial authority been so roundly criticized. One hears again the familiar echo: 'Curb that Court before it destroys the nation.' Bring the Justices down from 'the pedestal of fetish and deal with them as men and not supermen.' " Mason, *The Supreme Court from Taft to Warren*, at 4.

361. C. Herman Pritchett, *Congress Versus the Supreme Court, 1957-1960* (Minneapolis: University of Minnesota Press, 1961).

362. See Galloway, *The Second Period of the Warren Court: The Liberal Trend Abates (1957-1961)*, 19 Santa Clara L. Rev. 947 (1979).

363. 4 Friedman & Israel, *The Justices of the United States*, at 2896.

364. Lerner v. Casey, 357 U.S. 468 (1958); Beilan v. Board of Pub. Educ., 357 U.S. 299 (1958).

In 1959, the Court upheld contempt of Congress convictions for refusal to answer questions regarding communist activity[365] and for refusal to produce a guest list for an alleged "communist front" summer camp.[366] Again, in 1960, the Court sustained the discharge of a social worker for refusing to answer questions before the House Un-American Activities Committee.[367] In short, as Stanford political scientist Jonathan Casper has stated, "The period of 1958-1961 saw the Court step back from much of the doctrine it had appeared to be developing in the 1956-1957 period."[368]

History remembers, however, that the Court soon stepped forward again. During the early 1960's, two events occurred that made possible the emergence of the advanced liberal judicial activism that has come to be known as the definitive characteristic of the "Warren Court." First, the nation at large shifted toward political liberalism and idealism. Manifestations of this trend included the election and presidency of John Fitzgerald Kennedy, the Civil Rights Movement, and Lyndon Johnson's Great Society programs (e.g., the 1964 Civil Rights Act and Economic Development Act). Second, changes in Court personnel gave the liberals a solid five-vote majority that remained unbroken until 1969. As a result of these two developments, the Supreme Court, for the first time since its inception, actually became the active champion of the poor; not only resisting efforts to exploit the poor, but also initiating new programs for their benefit.[369]

The Court's retreat into conservatism was definitively halted in 1962 when the conservative Frankfurter retired and was replaced by the liberal Arthur Goldberg (1962-65),[370] a former counsel for the United Steelworkers and the AFL-CIO. Goldberg provided the Bench's activist wing with the dependable additional vote needed for a consistent majority.[371] In ad-

---

365. Barenblatt v. United States, 360 U.S. 109 (1959).

366. Uphaus v. Wyman, 360 U.S. 72 (1959).

367. Nelson v. City of Los Angeles, 362 U.S. 1 (1960).

368. Jonathan D. Casper, *The Politics of Civil Liberties* (New York: Harper & Row, 1972), at 75.

369. *See* Galloway, *The Third Period of the Warren Court: Liberal Dominance (1962-1969)*, 20 Santa Clara L. Rev. 773 (1980).

370. Goldberg was "one of the most activist-liberal judges ever to occupy a seat on the Court." Casper, *The Politics of Civil Liberties*, at 80.

371. The Goldberg appointment also brought the Court to perhaps the most liberal posture since its inception in 1790, surpassing the previous high point that had been set by the Black, Douglas, Murphy, Rutledge Court of the mid-1940's.

dition, that same year, Byron R. White (1962-), a moderate conservative with liberal leanings in civil rights matters, was selected to replace the conservative Charles E. Whittaker. Next, in 1965, Goldberg resigned to accept a position at the United Nations and was replaced by another staunch liberal, Abe Fortas (1965-69).[372] Finally, in 1967, the moderate conservative Clark was succeeded by Thurgood Marshall (1967-), who had been lead counsel in a number of major civil rights cases, including *Brown v. Board of Education*.[373] Thus, by 1967, the Court had attained another unprecedented historic plateau with six liberals, two moderates, and one conservative. The line-up now looked like this:

TABLE V

Alignment of Justices - 1967 to 1969

Liberal	Moderate	Conservative
Douglas	White	Harlan
Warren	Stewart	
Brennan		
Marshall		
Fortas		
Black[374]		

Numerous cases are available to illustrate the Warren Court's willingness to assist the poor in their struggle for economic and social justice. First, consider the core area of poverty law, government benefit programs. According to prior law, statutorily mandated financial assistance to the needy, such as unemployment compensation, disability allowances, old age benefits, aid to the blind, and aid to families with dependent children, were "privileges" that the government

---

372. Fortas was a New Dealer who had been a protege of William O. Douglas at Yale Law School and later at the SEC. He was counsel for petitioner in the great case, Gideon v. Wainwright, 372 U.S. 335 (1963).

373. 347 U.S. 483 (1954). Marshall was chief counsel for the NAACP Legal Defense Fund from 1938 to 1961.

374. Actually Black shifted into a relatively moderate position during the 1966-71 period, so his placement in the liberal wing is subject to some dispute. Even if Black is counted as a moderate, the liberals had an absolute five-vote majority.

was not compelled to grant and could therefore cut off without warning or justification. The Warren Court, in a move typical of its activist phase, rejected the right-privilege distinction and held that persons who qualify for these programs acquire a legally protected "property" interest in their benefits that cannot be taken away without due process of law.[375]

In general, welfare recipients received sympathetic treatment from the Warren Court. Although the number of welfare cases at bar was small, those that were decided usually went in favor of the recipients.[376] Moreover, toward the end of the decade, the Court appeared to be moving toward formal recognition of the principle that economic subsistence benefits are a fundamental right and that poverty as a classification is legally suspect, thus making the denial of benefits a matter for "strict judicial scrutiny."[377] Encouraged by the Warren Court's decisions, legal services attorneys developed an entire bustling field of activity known as welfare reform litigation and initiated many successful suits to correct deficiencies in the public welfare system.

Another line of rulings that illustrate the Warren Court's role as protector of the poor concerns publicly financed assistance for indigent criminal defendants.[378] These cases were based upon the recognition that, because they could not afford to pay the requisite legal fees, poor people were simply unable to obtain fair trials. The seminal case in this development, *Griffin v. Illinois* (1956),[379] has already been mentioned.[380] Among the many progeny of *Griffin*, the most

375. Sniadach v. Family Finance Corp., 395 U.S. 337 (1969) (holding that pre-trial garnishment without a prior hearing violates due process). See William Reich, *The New Property*, 73 Yale L.J. 733 (1969).

376. *E.g.*, Shapiro v. Thompson, 394 U.S. 618 (1969) (public assistance residency requirement held unconstitutional); King v. Smith, 392 U.S. 309 (1968) (denial of public assistance based on presence of "man assuming role of spouse" held illegal). The reason few cases were decided is that the legal program initiated by the Economic Development Act of 1964 was just getting underway in the late 1960's, and welfare reform cases were slow in working their way through the lower courts.

377. Shapiro v. Thompson, 394 U.S. 618 (1969), and Hunter v. Erickson, 393 U.S. 385 (1969), are usually cited as the cases which came closest to accepting these theories.

378. An even better known series of Warren Court cases increased the procedural protections of all criminal defendants whether rich or poor. Since poverty is the greater breeder of crime, these cases tended to assist the poor more than the rich. The discussion here, however, focuses on the narrower line of cases that are concerned specifically with impoverished defendants.

379. 351 U.S. 12 (1956).

380. *See* p. 157 *supra*.

famous was *Douglas v. California*,[381] which held that the state must provide indigent defendants with free counsel on appeal. By the end of Warren's tenure, the so-called *Griffin-Douglas* rule had generated a substantial body of decisions implementing the general concept that the kind of trial an individual receives should not depend on the amount of money he has.

Another example of the Warren Court's activism on behalf of indigent criminal defendants was *Gideon v. Wainwright* (1963),[382] which held that indigent defendants are entitled, under the sixth amendment, to free court-appointed attorneys in felony trials. The ruling, obviously, was a direct attempt to aid the poor and betokened a willingness to move into new areas and there create new legal rules for the protection of the poor.

A third illustration of the Warren majority's empathy with the poor is the liberal and activist stance taken in civil rights litigation. In some instances, the Bench directly and explicitly attempted to insure that poor persons are not deprived of important rights because of their poverty. For example, in *Harper v. Virginia Bd. of Elections* (1966),[383] the majority held that the right to vote may not be conditioned upon the payment of a poll tax since such a tax would deter indigent persons from exercising their franchise. In other instances, the Warren Court's assistance to the poor was more indirect, though, in the long run, perhaps of greater importance. For example, in response to the needs of citizens who suffered economic disadvantages as a result of racial and ethnic discrimination, the Warren Court both developed new law on its own initiative and broadly construed the power of Congress to deal with racial discrimination.[384] The classic instance of the Justices' taking the initiative was *Brown v. Board of Education*[385] which overturned the separate but equal doctrine that had been dominant in educational institutions since the 1890's.

Finally, the Warren Court accorded Congress vast and unprecedented powers to prohibit private racial discrimination. During the 1960's, the majority upheld Congress' authority,

---

381. 372 U.S. 353 (1963).
382. 372 U.S. 335 (1963); *see* Anthony Lewis, *Gideon's Trumpet* (New York: Vintage Books, 1964), for a detailed account of this famous case.
383. 383 U.S. 663 (1966).
384. *See* Cox, *The Warren Court*, at 24-70.
385. 347 U.S. 483 (1954).

under the commerce clause and section 5 of the Constitution's fourteenth amendment, to enact the Civil Rights Act of 1964, which prohibited racial discrimination in employment, housing, and public accomodations.[386] And, in a striking move, the Court resurrected the long dead Civil Rights Act of 1866 by finding that Congress was empowered under the thirteenth amendment to prohibit private discrimination.[387] Armed with these decisions, civil rights advocates proceeded with intense litigation on behalf of minorities, particularly in the fields of employment and education.[388]

Overall, the Justices serving for most of the 1960's reflected in their thinking a more advanced form of economic liberalism than had ever previously occurred in United States Supreme Court history. Prior to 1937, economic liberalism on the Supreme Court generally meant only a willingness to allow other branches of government to take action on behalf of the financially disadvantaged. This outlook left little room for positive effort by the Justices to advance the interests of the destitute and needy. Indeed, many of the earlier "liberal" jurists were politically and economically conservative in their personal viewpoints and exerted a liberal influence only because of their commitment to the concept of judicial restraint.[389] Conversely, judicial activism prior to 1937 was associated with economic conservatism and took the form of Justices' voting to nullify economic reform legislation.

After 1937, the Court liberals embraced the policy of judicial activism and the conservatives took the cause of restraint.[390] From 1962 to 1969, the activists had their period of greatest dominance while viewing themselves as the protector of the helpless rather than the protector of the rich. And for the first time in the nation's history, the Court majority began to exercise initiative on behalf of the poor.

---

386. Heart of Atlanta Motel v. United States, 379 U.S. 241 (1964).

387. Jones v. Alfred H. Mayer Co., 392 U.S. 409 (1968).

388. Another area in which the economic liberalism of the Warren Court was evident was antitrust, in which the password became "the government always wins." United States v. Von's Grocery Co., 384 U.S. 270, 301 (1966) (dissenting opinion of Stewart, J.).

389. The classic examples are Holmes and Stone.

390. The new pattern was strikingly illustrated by Felix Frankfurter, who presents a reverse image of Holmes and Stone. Frankfurter, an individual with deeply liberal personal convictions, became the functional arch-conservative of the Warren Court due to his commitment to the doctrine of judicial restraint.

Part Six

The Third Conservative Era (1969-)

Chapter Fifteen

The Burger Court (1969-)[391]

As the 1960's waned, the political mood of the American voter again shifted, this time sharply to the right. As the decade progressed, a growing polarization occurred within the populace. The pronounced liberalism of the early 1960's had been sustained by a wave of idealism. The Kennedy administration - with its youth, vigor, and intelligence - raised hopes that major socio-economic reform could be accomplished and fostered illusions that a new period of harmony and justice was dawning. Reformers believed that "we shall overcome" racial discrimination, poverty, and the competitive dog-eat-dog values of the old Adam Smith model of capitalism. Idealism was particularly strong among the young, who felt that organizing and demonstrating could help put an end to the unjust and destructive features of the established order.

In the latter half of the sixties, the wave ebbed. Innocence was lost. The freedom rides and sit-ins produced some worthwhile results, but they also precipitated an intense backlash of bigotry and attempted repression. The same political leaders who spoke of the Great Society let the nation fall deeper and deeper into the unpopular war in Vietnam that mocked the idealism felt by the reformers and led to bitter disillusionment. Clearly, the roots of the systemic injustice that the "movement" was attempting to change were deeper and more intractable than many expected. The encounter with unyielding resistance gave rise to anger on the part of some of the reformers.

---

391. This period is too recent to be discussed objectively as history. It is too early to tell which cases embody the beginnings of major trends and which cases are only aberrations. Nevertheless, to complete the story of this book, some facts and opinions will be set forth.

As it became increasingly apparent the establishment was not going to change its practices, anger burst into violence. Riots rocked the ghettoes across the nation. Reformers became revolutionaries. Nonviolence yielded to terror tactics. This, in turn, intensified the backlash that produced such extreme manifestations at Cicero, Kent State, and the tumultuous 1968 Chicago Democratic Convention.

The event that, more than any other, turned the tide against the spirit of reform and brought slightly more than 30 years of judicial liberalism to a close was Richard Nixon's 1968 election to the White House. The narrow margin of Nixon's victory over the liberal Minnesota Senator Hubert Humphrey suggests that the nation's political mood had still not swung drastically to conservatism before late 1968. When Nixon became President, however, the defeat of the reform movement became evident. His administration quickly applied its great skill in the use of the communications media to mobilize the backlash and encourage the repressive side of the "silent majority." Law and order were now the passwords,[392] and further reform efforts were to be suppressed. These developments were epitomized by the formulation of the Huston Plan[393] and the massive lock-up of anti-war marchers in Washington, D.C. in 1969.

This swing to the right in the nation at large was followed by one of the most dramatic short-term changes of judicial personnel in the entire history of the United States Supreme Court.[394] Within a stretch of approximately 30 months between the summer of 1969 and early 1972, the Court changed from a configuration of six liberals, two moderates, and one conservative[395] to a configuration of three liberals, two moderates,

---

392. As it turned out, the law and order standard was applied by the Nixon administration only to its opponents, not to its own members.

393. The Huston Plan was a blueprint drawn up by a member of the Nixon administration calling for a systematic assault by agencies of the federal government against dissidents. The plan contemplated large-scale domestic surveillance, infiltration of dissident groups, and suppression of protests.

394. Other such short-term changes on the Court include the seating of Barbour and Taney in 1837; the appointments of Fuller (1888) and Brewer (1890); the conservative appointments of the early 1920's; the Roosevelt appointments following the revolution of 1937; the 1949 replacement of Murphy and Rutledge by Clark and Minton, and the 1962 Frankfurter-Goldberg succession. None of these was more decisive than the shift that occurred in the 1969-1972 period.

395. If Black is counted as a moderate because of his shift to the right in the 1966-71 period, the split is 5-3-1- rather than 6-2-1.

and four conservatives. In June 1969, the liberal activists enjoyed an unbeatable six-vote majority.[396] By January 7, 1972, it was difficult for the liberals to win any controversial case before this Bench.

The change began in 1968 when liberal judicial strategists committed a monumental blunder. Realizing the 1968 election was in doubt, and applying a tactic the conservatives had used well in 1801, the liberals devised a plan to secure their dominance on the Court. Earl Warren would retire. President Johnson would appoint Associate Justice Abe Fortas to his position. Another liberal would be selected to take Fortas' seat. After Warren announced his intent to retire, however, an enormous problem arose. Fortas was attacked during his confirmation hearings for accepting a substantial honorarium from financier Lewis Wolfson while on the Court. Under pressure, Fortas resigned. Thus, instead of a relatively young liberal Chief Justice, plus five liberal Associates, Nixon inherited a Court with a lame duck Chief Justice, an open seat, and only four liberals.

Like William Howard Taft and Franklin Delano Roosevelt, Richard Milhouse Nixon was a political realist who was fully cognizant of the utility of having a Supreme Court that saw things his way. Therefore, he set out in a conscious and explicit fashion to find a new Chief and Associate Justice who shared his views regarding the nature of the Supreme Court and the meaning of the Constitution.[397] After making two nominations that were rejected by the Senate,[398] Nixon successfully appointed two conservative former corporate lawyers to the Bench, Chief Justice Warren E. Burger (1969-)[399] and Associate Justice Harry Blackmun (1970-),[400] a pair whose in-

---

396. This was the most liberal configuration in Supreme Court history to date. The Roosevelt Court had an eight-vote liberal wing in constitutional cases involving economic issues, but only four members of this group were crusading activists of the 1960's stripe.

397. The substance of these views will be discussed below.

398. The rejected appointees were Clement Haynesworth and the very conservative G. Harrold Carswell. These appointments made it clear that Nixon fully intended to end the activist era on the Court by packing it with conservatives.

399. Burger had practiced law for more than twenty years with a major corporate law firm in St. Paul and then, after three years with the Justice Department, had become a member of the conservative wing of the D.C. Circuit Court of Appeals. He had the most conservative voting record on the Court during his first Term and later settled into the position of the Court's second most conservative Justice behind William H. Rehnquist.

400. Although not as conservative as Burger, Blackmun was a core conservative

itial views were so closely aligned that they soon became known, in reference to their common home state, as the "Minnesota Twins." Thus, scarcely a year after Nixon took office, he had already managed to alter the balance of power on the Court dramatically.

The waning of the Warren Court then proceeded a step farther when Justices Black and Harlan retired in September 1971. Nixon's replacements for them were Lewis F. Powell, Jr. (1972-),[401] a corporate attorney from Richmond, Virginia, and William H. Rehnquist (1972-),[402] an arch-conservative former Phoenix attorney who immediately established himself on the Court's far right beyond even Chief Justice Burger. With the seating of Powell and Rehnquist, the composition of the Court looked like this:

TABLE W

Alignment of Justices - 1972 to 1975

Liberal	Moderate	Conservative
Douglas	Stewart	Rehnquist
Brennan	White	Burger
Marshall		Powell
		Blackmun

Clearly the days of liberal dominance were finished.

President Nixon, as has been said, explicitly let it be known that he would choose Justices who shared his views on constitutional adjudication. What were his views with regard to the rich-poor issue? The basic concept was that the Court should be restrained rather than activist and that it should not exercise so much initiative or leadership in attempting to rectify economic inequality. In his campaign, Nixon pledged "to

---

throughout the early 1970's wih the possible exception of the October 1974 Term, when he voted in a more moderate fashion. Later, he arguably became a moderate conservative.

401. Powell promptly became one of the Court's core conservatives and has remained a member of the conservative wing, with the possible exception of the October 1977 Term when he shifted toward a moderate position.

402. Rehnquist has been the Court's most conservative member each Term since he arrived on the Bench.

nominate to the Supreme Court individuals who shared my judicial philosophy, which is basically a conservative philosophy."[403]

This plan for the judiciary was but one component of Nixon's general political program. Nixon saw his role in history - at least in the realm of domestic politics - as being the destroyer of the New Deal. For too long, he believed, the federal government had extended its economic control over the people and, especially, the business corporations of the nation. Now, by forging a new and invincible political coalition out of the silent majority who still believed in free enterprise and the traditional moral order, Nixon would reverse history and dismantle the welfare state. One of the most striking manifestations of this program was Nixon's direct attempt to weaken the legal services and community action programs that had been the main components of the war on poverty initiated under President Johnson.[404]

The conservative effect of Nixon's appointments was felt immediately. Already during the October 1969 Supreme Court Term, the first post-Warren Term, judicial sentiment shifted perceptibly to the right.[405] During the following Term, the trend continued and the conservatives established a dominance that would remain unbroken through the decade and into the 1980's. The conservative outlook was so preponderant, in fact, that the liberal Douglas dissented in 50.7 percent of the cases decided in the October 1972 Term.[406]

Moreover, the "Nixon Court" gave prompt notice in its decisions that the Bench's egalitarian revolution was over. The leading ideas of the then emerging egalitarian legal theory were that welfare assistance is a fundamental right, that poverty is a

---

403. Richard M. Nixon, *Public Papers of The President* (Washington, D.C.: United States Government Printing Office), at 1055.

404. For example, Nixon appointed as director of the Office of Economic Opportunity, Howard Phillips, an ardent opponent of the war on poverty. The purpose of this appointment was to destroy the OEO, not to administer it.

405. *See* Galloway, *The First Decade of the Burger Court: Conservative Dominance (1969-1979)*, 21 Santa Clara L. Rev. 891. 893-97 (1981).

406. During the October 1972 Term the three liberal Warren Court holdovers (Douglas, Brennan, and Marshall) dissented together in no fewer than 43 cases, and Douglas dissented in 71 of the 140 cases decided during the Term. In contrast, the conservatives Blackmun and Burger dissented only 12 and 19 times respectively.

legally suspect classification,[407] and that legislation imposing burdens on the poor is subject to strict judicial scrutiny as regards its constitutionality. The Burger Court promptly rejected these ideas. In *Dandridge v. Williams* (1970),[408] the Court held that legislation affecting the rights of welfare recipients is subject only to the deferential rational basis test like other forms of economic regulation. Applying this test, the Court upheld a statutory ceiling on the amount of Aid to Families with Dependent Children (AFDC) benefits allowable for one family, regardless of the number of children. On the same day in 1970, in *Rosado v. Wyman*,[409] the majority sustained a statute imposing "percentage reductions" of welfare grants below state-determined need. *Dandridge* and *Rosado* were watershed cases indicating that a chill had descended upon the area of welfare reform through constitutional litigation.[410]

Any doubt about the Nixon Court's determination to retrench in the area of poverty law was removed over the next few years. In 1971, *James v. Valtierra*[411] upheld a California constitutional provision requiring approval by local referendum before installation of low rent housing within a community. Here was a clear case of discrimination against the poor. No referenda were required for normal housing; they were only mandated for housing for the poor. Applying the deferential rational basis test, the Court found this type of discrimination permissible, thus inflicting a major defeat on low-income persons in their efforts to live outside ghettoes.

The case that perhaps best symbolizes the Court's retreat on the rich/poor issue from the liberalism of the 1960's is *San Antonio Independent School Dist. v. Rodriguez* (1973),[412] the

---

407. A suspect classification is a constitutionally disfavored classification that is subject to strict scrutiny rather than the deferential rational basis test that usually applies in equal protection cases. Race is the most suspect of all classifications. Sex is a "semi-suspect" classification.

408. 397 U.S. 471 (1970).

409. 397 U.S. 397 (1970).

410. *Cf.* Edelman v. Jordan, 415 U.S. 651 (1974) (holding that the eleventh amendment bars an order requiring retroactive welfare payments); Board of Regents v. Roth, 408 U.S. 564 (1972), and Perry v. Sinderman, 408 U.S. 593 (1972) (which undercut the foundations of the "new property"); Wyman v. James, 400 U.S. 309 (1971) (upholding "home visits" of welfare recipients).

411. 402 U.S. 137 (1971).

412. 411 U.S. 1 (1973).

widely publicized and debated school finance case. The controversy here involved a challenge to Texas' system for financing public education which, because it was based in large part on property taxes, had given rise to extreme differences in the amount of money available per child in rich and poor districts. Again, the Nixon Court made it clear that the days of liberal activism on behalf of the poor were over. Since in the view of Powell, Burger, Blackmun, Rehnquist, and Stewart, the Texas school financing system was not without some rational foundation, it was constitutional.[413] The result of the decision was to leave in effect a system that provided more money for the education of children in wealthy districts than in poor districts and thus contributed to the perpetuation of the cycle of poverty by insuring that economically deprived children receive lower quality education. Under Warren, the decision would have gone the other way.[414]

Then, in 1974, the Court signalled the end of the egalitarian revolution on behalf of indigent criminal defendants. That year, in *Ross v. Moffitt*,[415] the Court restricted the reigning *Griffin-Douglas* rule[416] by holding that the Constitution's equal protection clause only requires that indigents be provided with an adequate opportunity for a fair adjudication. If this standard is met, the majority opinion concluded, the Warren Court principle that the kind of justice a person receives should not depend on the amount of money he has is inapplicable. On this basis, the majority concluded that the government need not assign attorneys to indigent criminal defendants to help prepare petitions for discretionary review of their convictions in either state or federal supreme courts.[417] Also in

---

413. In reaching the conclusion that the rational basis test was controlling rather than the strict scrutiny test, the Court made two additional conservative decisions: (1) that the right to equal opportunity is not a fundamental right and (2) that the classification of students on the basis of the value of property holdings within the school district is not a suspect classification.

414. The Court did not entirely abandon the concept that poverty is an inadequate basis for denying important rights. *See, e.g.,* Bullock v. Carter, 405 U.S. 134 (1972) (impoverished candidates for office need not pay filing fee); Tate v. Short, 401 U.S. 395 (1971) (persons may not be made to serve jail sentences simply because they are too poor to pay criminal fines); Williams v. Illinois, 399 U.S. 235 (1970) (same).

415. 417 U.S. 600 (1974).

416. The *Griffin-Douglas* rule requires the government to provide free assistance for indigent criminal defendants. *See* p. 157, 161-62 *supra.*

417. Other illustrative decisions in the early 1970's adversely affecting the poor included Ortwein v. Schwab, 410 U.S. 656 (1973) (upholding a filing fee for appeals from welfare rul-

1974, the Nixon Court held that states may require repayment of costs of services provided to indigent criminal defendants in spite of the apparent chilling effect of such a requirement on the exercise of constitutional rights.[418]

The following year, judicial liberalism suffered still another setback when Justice Douglas, the Court's most liberal member for more than two decades, was forced to resign because of illness. Ironically, the choice of Douglas' replacement fell to President Gerald Ford, who had led an earlier congressional effort to impeach Douglas. Ford selected John Paul Stevens, another former corporation lawyer and a moderate.[419] Stevens' arrival left the following line-up on the Bench:

TABLE X
Alignment of Justices - 1975

Liberal	Moderate	Conservative
Brennan	White	Rehnquist
Marshall	Stewart	Burger
	Stevens	Powell
		Blackmun

After the seating of Stevens, the Burger Court continued its conservative retrenchment in many areas affecting the poor. Welfare recipients lost a number of tough cases including some in which basic constitutional rights were clearly at stake.[420] Indigent criminal defendants found their rights to public assistance in presenting their defenses further circumscribed.[421] In the antitrust field, the rule of thumb

---

ings); United States v. Kras, 409 U.S. 434 (1973) (upholding a filing fee for bankruptcy proceedings); Lindsey v. Normet, 405 U.S. 56 (1972) (holding housing not to be a fundamental right).

418. Fuller v. Oregon, 417 U.S. 40 (1974).

419. Stevens began his career as a moderate. In fact, he was closer to Brennan and Marshall than to Rehnquist and Burger during his first full Term. Thereafter he shifted toward the right into a position very near to the center of the Court.

420. E.g., Trainor v. Hernandez, 431 U.S. 434 (1977) (holding that federal courts may not enjoin an unconstitutional attachment of credit union funds owned by person accused of welfare fraud); Simon v. Eastern Kentucky Welfare Rights Org., 426 U.S. 26 (1976) (rejecting respondents' standing to sue).

421. E.g. Scott v. Illinois, 440 U.S. 367 (1979) (denying appointed counsel to indigent defendants in cases not involving imprisonment.

changed from "the government always wins" to "the government always loses."[422] Racial minorities suffered a series of defeats that seriously impaired the ability of federal district courts to combat racial discrimination.[423] The Court imposed new procedural rules that created major barriers to public interest litigation.[424]

In general, the economic conservatism of the Burger Court, during its first decade, was carried out through procedural rulings, statutory interpretation, and constitutional restraint rather than activism. For the most part, the Bench did not return to the constitutional conservative activism that was the hallmark of its pre-1937 legacy. As the years passed, however, the Court majority did issue a few major decisions involving constitutional censorship of economic legislation. Four cases are especially noteworthy.

The first and most famous of the series was *National League of Cities v. Usery*,[425] which reactivated the tenth amendment as a limit on federal power to regulate the conduct of state and local governments. In this widely noted 5-4 decision, the Court struck down minimum wage/maximum hour legislation for public employees as a violation of state autonomy and, in the process, overruled a major Warren Court ruling that had gone the other way.[426] A second important case was *First Nat'l Bank v. Bellotti* (1978),[427] which held that the first amendment pro-

---

422. *E.g.*, Earl E. Pollock, *Antitrust, the Supreme Court, and the Spirit of '76*, 72 Northwestern Univ. L. Rev. 631 (1977).

423. *E.g.*, Dayton Bd. of Educ. v. Brinkman, 433 U.S. 406 (1977) (restricting remedies in school desegregation cases); International Brotherhood of Teamsters v. United States, 431 U.S. 324 (1977) (signalling the end of liberal activism in employment discrimination cases); Washington v. Davis, 426 U.S. 229 (1976) (holding that the equal protection clause prohibits only intentional racial discrimination); Rizzo v. Goode, 423 U.S. 362 (1976) (holding that a claim of racial harassment by Philadelphia police does not present a justiciable case).

424. *E.g.*, Trainor v. Hernandez, 431 U.S. 434 (1977) (expanding the doctrine of federal court abstention); Piper v. Chris-Craft Indus. Inc., 430 U.S. 1 (1977) (narrowing implied private causes of action under federal statutes); Simon v. Eastern Kentucky Welfare Rights Org., 426 U.S. 26 (1976) (restricting standing of public interest groups to challenge illegal practices); Warth v. Seldin, 422 U.S. 490 (1975) (same); Alyeska Pipeline Serv. Co. v. Wilderness Society, 421 U.S. 240 (1975) (rejecting awards of attorneys' fees to successful plaintiffs absent express statutory authorization); Eisen v. Carlisle & Jacquelin, 417 U.S. 156 (1974) (requiring plaintiffs to pay for notice to members of plaintiffs' class).

425. 426 U.S. 833 (1976).

426. *Maryland v. Wirtz*, 392 U.S. 183 (1968). *National League of Cities* is the most recent in the long line of fair labor standards cases that have provided so many important examples in earlier chapters. These cases include *Lochner* (1905), *Muller* (1908), *Bunting* (1917), *Adkins* (1923), *Tipaldo* (1937), *Parrish* (1937), and *Wirtz* (1968).

427. 435 U.S. 765 (1978).

hibits states from restricting corporate expenditures designed to influence the outcome of referendum elections. Political speech is entitled to full first amendment protection, the five-vote majority held, regardless of whether its source is an individual or a business corporation. *Bellotti* was the foremost in a string of cases restricting government power to control political speech by corporations.[428]

The remaining two cases resuscitated the contract clause as a potentially formidable barrier to economic reform legislation. In *United States Trust Co. v. New Jersey* (1977),[429] a 4-3 majority held that New York and New Jersey could not repeal a covenant banning the use of bond revenues to subsidize rail passenger transportation. This decision undercut the states' ability to respond to the energy crunch common in the 1970's by shifting funds into mass transit facilities. Finally, in *Allied Structural Steel Co. v. Spannaus* (1978),[430] a five-vote majority held that the contract clause prohibited Minnesota from requiring employers who leave the state to pay assessments designed to insure pension benefits for former employees. Brennan's dissent bitterly criticized the decision, claiming that it threatened "to undermine the jurisprudence of property rights developed over the last 40 years."[431]

In 1981, the most recent change in Supreme Court personnel brought the first woman Justice to the Bench. Potter Stewart, a moderate-conservative, resigned at the end of October 1980 Term. To replace him, President Reagan nominated Sandra Day O'Connor, a "Goldwater Republican" from Arizona and a former Stanford Law School classmate of Justice Rehnquist. O'Connor's voting record during her first year of service suggests that she is a member of the Court's conservative wing. Already, the phrase "Arizona Twins" is being used to refer to her and Rehnquist.[432]

Blackmun, meanwhile, has moved out of the core conservative bloc and into a more moderate position. The following table reflects these recent changes:

---

428. *E.g.*, Consolidated Edison Co. v. Public Serv. Comm'n, 447 U.S. 530 (1980); Buckley v. Valeo, 424 U.S. 1 (1976).

429. 431 U.S. 1 (1977).

430. 438 U.S. 234 (1978).

431. *Id.* at 259.

432. "And Now, The Arizona Twins," *Time*, April 19, 1982, at 49.

TABLE Y

Alignment of Justices - October 1982 Term

Liberal	Moderate	Conservative
Brennan	Blackmun	Rehnquist
Marshall	White	Burger
	Stevens	Powell
		O'Connor

If O'Connor remains with the conservatives, an apt nickname for the bloc may be the "four horsepersons." Regardless, it seems likely that the Stewart/O'Connor succession has pushed the already conservative Burger Court even farther to the right and has made the prospects for the poor at the bar of the Supreme Court poor indeed.

Conclusions

The first major conclusion suggested by this study is that the United States Supreme Court is and always has been a political body which decides cases on the basis of socio-economic values rather than value-neutral legal rules. This fact has been recognized by legal scholars and practitioners for years, but it tends to be overlaid by the myth that judges are merely technicians who discover and apply the law in an objective manner. The data from Supreme Court history suggest that the myth is entirely untrue.

From the very start, Presidents have selected Justices primarily because of their economic and political views. This has been so for Washington, Jefferson, Lincoln, Taft, Wilson, Roosevelt, Nixon and many others. Moreover, once on the Court, the Justices have tended to vote repeatedly in tightly-knit blocs on the main economic issues, so that constitutional adjudication becomes largely a matter of political head-counting similar to the decision making process in the House and Senate, rather than a quest for the single correct and just answer to legal problems. Indeed, a characteristic of most issues regarding the distribution of wealth is that exhaustive and fully rational philosophies exist to justify both the conservative and liberal viewpoints. Thus, in close cases, the decision will depend primarily on the preferences of the Justices and will not be controlled by objective inquiry into legal principles.

It should be noted, however, that, although Justices are political animals selected largely on the basis of their political and economic beliefs, Presidents have frequently been disappointed in the judicial performance of their appointees. The future behavior of Supreme Court Justices has proved to be somewhat unpredictable. James Madison's selection of the conservative Story was the first major presidential mistake of this nature. Theodore Roosevelt's frustration at Holmes' refusal to enforce antitrust laws vigorously is notorious. Wilson's error in nominating McReynolds was fatal to the prospects for a truly progressive Court in the World War One era. And Eisenhower's disgust at Warren's liberal-activism is well known. Nevertheless, despite these exceptions, Presidents have usually done rather well in selecting Justices whose views on major issues matched their own. Washington, Jackson, Harding, Franklin Roosevelt, and Nixon, for example, succeeded in creating new Courts - indeed new eras of Supreme Court history - that reflected their political and economic views.

Another conclusion suggested by the historical materials covered in this book is that none of the common images regarding the role of the Supreme Court is adequate to cover the Court's entire history. The Court changes. It is a shapeshifter which, at times, has resembled each of three different profiles. It has been a servant of the rich, a champion of the poor, *and* a neutral mediator among interest groups.

During the first conservative era (1790-1835), the Court functioned - albeit in a rather restrained way - as a protector of the wealthy classes. During the first liberal era (1836-1890), the Court assumed a role somewhat like that of a neutral mediator between the rich and the poor. Throughout much of this second period, the Court was perhaps more sympathetic with the needs of the poor. Nevertheless, the Court's personnel were recruited mainly from the class of corporate lawyers, so there was no shortage of empathy with the desires of expanding capitalism. Moreover, the Court certainly did not view itself as the "champion" of the poor or as the initiator of economic reform programs.

During the second conservative era (1890-1937), the Court assumed a role very close to that ascribed to it by its more aggressive left-wing critics, namely, handmaiden to the corporate rich. Starting in the 1890's, the Court undertook a campaign to prevent the people of the United States from making the structural changes necessary to bridge the gap from the frontier abundance of early America to the urban-industrial America of the twentieth century. This campaign was waged on behalf of the rich and was designed to prevent the people from regulating private wealth.

During the period after 1937, the Court largely returned to the role of mediator between conflicting interests. For a brief period in the 1960's, the Court began to resemble the third image and to function as champion of the poor. This phase in the Court's history was cut short by the judicial appointments and political trends of the Nixon period.

The longest portion of the Court's history (including the 93 years from 1790 to 1835 and 1890 to 1937) has been characterized by a definite partiality for the rich. To a large extent, this was the result of policies held by the "founding fathers" and written into the Constitution. It seems incontestable that the drafters of the Constitution intended to place the rights of private property in a preferred position and to assign to the Supreme Court the duty of guarding that position. In other words, there was an original *explicit* intention that the Court function as special protector of the wealthy. Thus, in order to transcend this role, the Court had to break away from the instructions contained in its own charter and redefine its purpose to fit changing social needs.

Even after the Court succeeded in breaking out of its original role as protector of the wealthy, it is clear that it did not, for the most part, function as champion of the poor. Of the three common images, this one is by far the least descriptive of the Court's actual behavior. Only during a relatively few years in the 1940's, 1950's, and 1960's did the Court become an advocate and initiator of economic reform, and the Burger Court has left no doubt that it considers the experiment to be at an end. In short, the Supreme Court has usually alternated between roles as protector of the rich and as neutral mediator and has only rarely assumed the role of champion of the poor.

Another major conclusion suggested by the historical materials is that the Court, for all its theoretical independence, is quite responsive to pressure from public opinion and from the political branches. From Marshall's suggestion that Congress be given power to reverse the Court's constitutional rulings to the Court's astonishing 1937 revolution in the face of FDR's Court-packing proposal and beyond, the Court has normally retreated when subjected to sustained majority opposition. Without the power of the purse or the gun, the Court is sustained only by public acceptance and therefore must normally stay within limits set by public opinion.

The Court has been able, on the one hand, to write the views of its controlling majority into law and, on the other hand, to stage orderly retreats in the face of strong public pressure largely because of the extraordinary flexibility of its doctrinal tools. In most cases, the Court has the sovereign prerogative of choice, as Cardozo put it. The Court is free to discard old rules and invent new ones when it wishes. Moreover, when it wants to preserve the illusion of continuity, the Court can make new law by gradually expanding or contracting existing rules so that the change is detectable only by lawyers. Thus, the Taft Court was able to restrict government's power to regulate prices simply by narrowing the definition of "businesses affected with a public interest." Even the famous constitutional revolution of 1937 left the old rational basis test in place, simply substituting a deferential approach for the conservative-activist approach that had characterized the pre-1937 Court.

In this regard, it is interesting to note that many of the major doctrines of Supreme Court law are double-edged and can be used, in different contexts, by conservatives and liberals alike to achieve their goals. During the first century and a half of Supreme Court history, for example, judicial activism was a tactic normally used to further conservative ends, and judicial restraint was the rallying cry of the liberals. In contrast, the post-1937 liberals took over the activist approach, and the conservatives increasingly adopted the Holmesian doctrine of judicial restraint. In short, once a legal doctrine has been developed, it takes on a life of its own and may be put to uses unforeseen by and even opposite to the desires of the original creators.

Similarly, history suggests that some major ideological issues are largely red herrings which conceal rather than reveal the realities that underlie the Court's decisions. Charles Warren, the leading Supreme Court historian, contended that the states' rights doctrine has been used in his manner.[433] According to Warren, concrete cases are normally decided on the

---

433. 1 Warren, *Supreme Court* at 388: "[T]hroughout American history, devotion to State-Rights and opposition to the jurisdiction of the Federal Government and the Federal Judiciary, whether in the South or the North, has been based, not so much on dogmatic political theories or beliefs, as upon the particular economic, political or social legislation which the decision of the Court happened to sustain or overthrow. No State and no section of the Union has found any difficulty in adopting or opposing the State-Rights theory, whenever its interests lay that way."

basis of whose ox is being gored, and states' rights arguments are invoked simply to provide an abstract rationalization for the result. Thus, the Jeffersonians invoked states' rights to prevent the federal government from favoring the rich, but the four horsemen used the same theory to curtail federal efforts to help the poor. In fact, Supreme Court history teaches that the verbiage in many Court opinions is merely a screen, and that the attentive student should look underneath the words to the economic effects that actually explain the outcome.

Whither the Court now? All available signals suggest that, in the short run, the Court is headed to the right. The strongest bloc on the present Court - the four horsepersons, Rehnquist, Burger, Powell, and O'Connor - are only one vote shy of a majority. In most cases, they can easily find the necessary vote and more among the three moderate conservatives, Blackmun, White, and Stevens. Moreover, if Brennan and Marshall, the tattered remnants of the once dominant liberal-activist wing, cannot outlast the Reagan presidency, we may soon have a Court without a liberal wing. In short, the Court's third conservative era may still have a long way to go before the pendulum begins to swing back in the other direction.

The possibility of a Court without liberals is not a happy one. The law works best when it embodies a sound compromise of valid but conflicting interests. The absence of a loyal opposition can truncate the necessary dialogue among competing viewpoints and lead to undesirable results. For optimum growth of legal doctrine, we need vigorous statements of both the thesis and antithesis in order to reach an adeqate synthesis. More important, in terms of social harmony, we need a balanced Court so that the legal system can encourage a process of orderly change and provide a lightning rod for draining off anger before it reaches revolutionary intensities.

In short, restraint and moderation are needed on the part of the conservative leaders who now dominate the presidency and Senate, the two arms of government which control future Court appointments. Consider the following likely scenario. What if the two remaining liberals, Brennan and Marshall, retire or die before 1985? If Reagan follows his arch-conservative instincts and the Republican-controlled Senate backs him, we are likely to have two more hard-line conservatives join the already dominant Burger-Rehnquist wing. William

Clark, Reagan's good friend and former right-wing California Supreme Court justice, might be one. And Robert Bork, conservative former Solicitor General, might be the second. After such changes the Court would look like this:

TABLE Z

Hypothetical Alignment of Justices - October 1984 Term

Liberal	Moderate	Conservative
	White	Rehnquist
	Stevens	Burger
	Blackmun	Clark
		Bork
		Powell
		O'Connor

Would this be good for the country? The answer seems to be plainly no. As Brandeis pointed out so many times, the greatest domestic danger to the stability of America's government is the failure of free enterprise capitalism to make the adjustments needed to cure real injustice and prevent the emergence of widespread, revolutionary dissatisfaction. Since 1968, the nation has increasingly turned its back on the poor. The tax revolt; the dismantling of the Great Society and the New Deal; the policy of increased welfare for the military-industrial complex and across-the-board cuts for the poor - all these will lead to a day of reckoning unless the main organs of government are perceived as fair and representative of the poor as well as the rich.

The time seems to be at hand for the Supreme Court to moderate its course and eschew the right-wing pattern that has increasingly characterized its third conservative era. Ironically, however, the main attacks on the Court are still coming from the right, and the Justices themselves are calling for less rather than more liberal-activism. The Nixon-Reagan agenda for the Court has worked too well, and it may soon be necessary to re-chisel the motto on the Court's pediment to read, "Justice for the rich." Let us hope sound judgment prevails and the Court once again resumes the balanced position needed to insure equal justice under law.

It is too early to tell whether the Warren Court's assumption of the role of special protector of the poor and disenfranchised was a passing aberration or a harbinger of things to come. History certainly suggests that the Supreme Court has a greater tendency toward economic conservatism than economic liberalism. Nevertheless, it is also true that the constitutional revolution of 1937 put an apparent end to the Court's career as censor of economic reform legislation and created a need for the Court to be reborn in a new image. Thus, the historical data from the pre-1937 period may be less relevant to the future of the Court than the new legal developments that began to emerge in the 1940's and 1960's.

If this is so, the future may show the Burger Court to be a historical anachronism and the Warren Court to be the bellwether of a new era in which the Supreme Court throws off its traditional aristocratic image and begins to make an active contribution to democratic government by protecting and advancing the interests of those groups who have traditionally been powerless and disenfranchised. In the short run, however, the Justices clearly favor the rich, and the best strategy for the advocates of the poor is to stay out of the Supreme Court as much as possible and to focus their economic reform efforts in the legislature.

INDEX